Contents

Awa' an' Bile yer Heid!

David Ross is a professional writer with a number of serious historical books to his credit. As a long-time observer of his fellow-Scots he has also written *Xenophobe's Guide to the Scots* and has compiled several anthologies of Scottish wit and humour. Among his current projects is one to have flyting restored as a national art form.

Rupert Besley has worked for 25 years as a freelance cartoonist illustrating books and drawing postcards of people not enjoying their holidays. His work has appeared in a variety of publications, including *Punch*, *The Oldie* and *Country Life*. He has written and illustrated a number of books of his own, including the bestselling *The Cannae Sutra: The Scots Joy of Sex*.

Awa' an' Bile yer Heid!

Scottish Insults and Curses

Compiled by David Ross

Illustrated by Rupert Besley

BIRLINN

This edition first published in 2007 by
Birlinn Limited
West Newington House
10 Newington Road
Edinburgh
EH9 1QS

www.birlinn.co.uk

First published in 1999 by Birlinn Limited

ISBN 13: 978 1 84158 594 9
ISBN 10: 1 84158 594 7

British Library Cataloguing-in-Publication Data
A catalogue record for this book is available from the British Library

Typeset by Iolaire Typesetting, Newtonmore
Printed and bound by
Cox & Wyman Ltd, Reading

Introduction

There is something peculiarly satisfying about an effective and well delivered insult – when it is applied to someone else, of course. The greatest satisfaction is to have created it, but to witness a good insult, or even to read it on the page, gives a certain kind of pleasure. It is a complex feeling, and when looked at closely, parts of it are not very nice, close to what Thomas Carlyle called 'mischief-joy', the pleasure in other people's troubles. But there can also be a feeling of relief – somebody else is being being got at; and sense of justice done – someone is getting a well-deserved come-uppance. A clever insult also gets admiration for wit and boldness. Like microbes that survive in a wide range of environments, insults can live anywhere on the line between extreme malevolence and a sort of half-contemptuous fondness. One of their justifications has always been that 'Sticks and stones will break your bones, but names will never harm you', but unfortunately this is not always true, and sometimes name-calling is the cause of physical violence. But this collection deals with the insult only as a long-established form of self-expression – almost a minor artform. It has absolutely no hostile intentions against any person, place or point of view.

If an international insult ratings table existed, one feels that Scotland would stand high – here at least is a game in which the country punches above its weight. For this, in part, the neighbouring nation must be thanked. England has provided ample opportunity to sharpen Scottish barbs over the past thousand years.

But the sincerest insults are always nearest to home; and the Scots have always been enthusiastic insulters of one another. Why should this be? Without probing too far into the murk of the national psyche, one might note a certain competitiveness, a capacity for abstract thought, a sense of community which could often be stifling. Genetic, cultural, even climatic factors all come into it, no doubt. When David Hume described his fellow countrymen as '. . . the rudest, perhaps, of all the European nations, the most necessitous, the most turbulent, and the most unsettled' (in a letter to Edward Gibbon of March 1776), he meant rude in the sense of rough, but it could equally have applied to their talk. A degree of refinement has crept in over the two hundred years plus since he wrote these words, and the Scots are no longer the most poverty-stricken Europeans; but, other things being equal, the great philosopher's words keep a certain truth.

Through the centuries, the Scots have found a great deal to be rude about, but in addition the collection covers insults to Scotland and the Scots (we were surprised, even sometimes indignant, to find not everyone liked us). Conveniently arranged under broad subject headings, in its own way it offers a modest insight into the national character. And so, happy reading, or browsing. If you don't like it – 'Awa' an' bile yer heid!'

Architecture and buildings

The Armadillo.

> A local name for the entrance hall of the Auditorium
> at the Scottish Exhibition & Conference Centre, Glasgow.

During a tour of New York, A.J. Balfour was shown over one of the city's tallest and most recent skyscrapers. He was told how much it had cost to build, how many men had been employed in its construction, how long it had taken to build, and how fast the lifts travelled.

'Dear me, how remarkable,' he murmured. Finally his guide informed him that the building was so solid that it would easily last for a thousand years.

'Dear, dear me, what a great pity.'

> Noted of ARTHUR JAMES BALFOUR (1848–1930),
> in K. Williams, *Acid Drops* (1980)

I am sorry to report the Scott Monument a failure. It is like the spire of a Gothic church taken off and stuck in the ground.

> CHARLES DICKENS (1812–70)

From my window I see the rectangular blocks of man's
Insolent mechanical ignorance rise, with hideous exactitude,
against the sun
against the sky.
It is the University.

> ALAN JACKSON (1938–), 'From My Window'

5

... the ceilings are so low all you can have for tea is kippers.

CHARLES MCKEAN, *The Scottish Thirties*, 1987, on bungalows

... a very strange house ... that it should ever have been lived in is the most astonishing, staggering, saddening thing of all. It is surely the strangest and saddest monument that Scott's genius created.

EDWIN MUIR (1887–1959), *Scottish Journey*, on Abbotsford

The rocks of the castle ... guide the eye to barracks at the top and cauliflowers at the bottom.

JOHN RUSKIN (1819-1900), *The Poetry of Architecture*,
on Edinburgh Castle

The wise people of Edinburgh built ... a small vulgar Gothic steeple on the ground and called it the Scott Monument.

JOHN RUSKIN (1819-1900), *The Poetry of Architecture*

Standing on the ramparts of Stirling Castle, the spectator cannot help noticing an unsightly excrescence of stone and lime rising on the brow of the Abbey Craig. This is the Wallace Tower.

ALEXANDER SMITH (1830–67), *A Summer in Skye*

Day by day, one new villa, one new object of offence, is added to another; all around Newington and Morningside, the dismallest structures keep springing up like mushrooms; the pleasant hills are loaded with them, each impudently squatted in its garden . . . They belong to no style of art, only to a form of business.

ROBERT LOUIS STEVENSON (1850–94),
Picturesque Notes on Edinburgh

At last I view the storied scene,
The embattled rock and valley green;
And hear, mid reverent nature's hush,
The water closet's frequent flush.

JOHN WARRACK, letter to *The Scotsman*
protesting against the building of a
public lavatory in Princes Street Gardens,
Edinburgh (December 1920)

Why do you propose these boxes for our people?

JOHN WHEATLEY (1873–1930),
on official standards for house-building, 1923

It is worse than ridiculous to see the people of Dumfries coming forward with their pompous mausoleum.

WILLIAM WORDSWORTH (1770–1850),
Letter to John Scott (1816),
on the Burns tomb in Dumfries

Those sunless courts, entered by needles' eyes of apertures, congested with hellish, heaven-scaling barracks, reeking with refuse and evil odours, inhabited promiscuously by poverty and prostitution.

ISRAEL ZANGWILL (1864–1926), on Edinburgh tenements (1895)

Art and artists

May the Devil fly away with the fine arts!

THOMAS CARLYLE (1795–1881), *Latter-Day Pamphlets*

. . . many of these artists in this exhibition seem to have an overt and blatant concern with money and, inevitably, status. They have dramatically reduced the scope and vision of their art so that it may become a saleable commodity, a potential piece of private property and a casual investment for Scotland's doomed and essentially philistine bourgeoisie.

KEN CURRIE, reviewing the exhibition 'Contemporary Art from Scotland' in *Stigma* 2 (1983)

Arts Councils are the insane asylums of bureaucracy.

IAN HAMILTON FINLAY (1925–2006),
'An Alphabet', *Studio International* (1981)

. . . the unfortunate monarch, whose head was executed as ruthlessly on canvas as she herself had been at Fotheringay

H. GREY GRAHAM, *The Social Life of Scotland in the Eighteenth Century* (1899), on posthumous portraits of Mary, Queen of Scots (1542–87)

'My dear Roberts,' wrote the critic in a private letter, 'you may have seen my remarks on your pictures. I hope they will make no difference to our friendship. Yours, etc.' 'My dear —,' wrote the painter in reply, 'the next time I meet you I shall pull your nose. I hope it will make no difference to our friendship. Yours, etc., D. Roberts.'

TOLD OF DAVID ROBERTS (1796–1864), in Alexander Hislop,
The Book of Scottish Anecdote

. . . the word 'art' in Scotland . . . a condensed expression for 'l'art de se faire ridicule'

JOHN RUSKIN (1819–1900), *The Poetry of Architecture*

Authors, critics and publishers

It is really very generous of Mr Thomson to consent to live at all.

Anonymous contemporary critic of James Thomson (1834–1882), poet of voluptuous death, quoted in notes to Douglas Young, *Scottish Verse 1851–1951*

Why bother yourself about the cataract of drivel for which Conan Doyle was responsible?

JOSEPH BELL (1837–1911), said to have been Conan Doyle's model for Sherlock Holmes, in a letter

The archetypal Scottish sexist.

ALAN BOLD (1943–98), *The Sensual Scot*, on Robert Burns

One good critic could demolish all this dreck, but one good critic is precisely what we do not have. Instead we are lumbered with pin-money pundits, walled-up academics or old ladies of both sexes.

EDDIE BOYD (1916–1989), on Scottish drama and drama critics, in *Cencrastus* (Autumn 1987)

'It adds a new terror to death.'

> LORD BROUGHAM (1778–1868), Lord Chancellor of Great Britain, on Lord Campbell's *Lives of the Lord Chancellors* (1845–47)

O thou whom poesy abhors,
Whom prose has turned out of doors!
Heardst thou that groan?
Proceed no farther:
'Twas laurelled Martial roaring murther.

> ROBERT BURNS (1759–1796), on James Elphinston's (1721–1809) translation of Martial's *Epigrams*

And think'st thou, Scott! by vain conceit perchance,
On public taste to foist thy stale romance . . .
No! when the sons of song descend to trade,
Their bays are sear, their former laurels fade.
Let such forgo the poet's sacred name,
Who rack their brains for lucre, not for fame.

> LORD BYRON (1788–1824), *English Bards and Scotch Reviewers*, on Sir Walter Scott

My northern friends have accused me, with justice, of personality towards their great literary anthropophagus, Jeffrey; but what else was to be done with him and his dirty pack, who feed by 'lying and slandering' and slake their thirst with 'evil speaking?'

> LORD BYRON, postscript to the second edition of *English Bards and Scotch Reviewers*, on Francis Jeffrey and the *Edinburgh Review*

Napoleon is a tyrant, a monster, the sworn foe of our nation. But gentlemen – he once shot a publisher.

THOMAS CAMPBELL (1777–1844), proposing a toast to
Napoleon Bonaparte at a writers' dinner

Fricassee of dead dog ... A truly unwise little book. The kind of man that Keats was gets ever more horrible to me. Force of hunger for pleasure of every kind, and want of all other force – such a soul, it would once have been very evident, was a chosen 'vessel of Hell'.

THOMAS CARLYLE (1795–1881), on Monckton Milnes's *Life of Keats*

A weak, diffusive, weltering, ineffectual man ... Never did I see such apparatus got ready for thinking, and so little thought. He mounts scaffolding, pulleys and tackle, gathers all the tools in the neighbourhood with labour, with noise, demonstration, precept, abuse, and sets – three bricks.

THOMAS CARLYLE (1795–1881), on Samuel Taylor Coleridge

A more pitiful, rickety, gasping, staggering, stammering Tom-fool I do not know. Poor Lamb! Poor England! when such a despicable abortion is given the name of genius.

THOMAS CARLYLE (1795–1881), on Charles Lamb

Shelley is a poor creature, who has said or done nothing worth a serious man being at the trouble of remembering.

THOMAS CARLYLE (1795–1881), on Percy Bysshe Shelley

At bottom, this Macaulay is but a poor creature with his dictionary literature and erudition, his saloon arrogance. He has no vision in him. He will neither see nor do any great thing.

THOMAS CARLYLE (1795–1881), on Lord Macaulay

. . . standing in a cess-pool, and adding to it

THOMAS CARLYLE (1795–1881), quoted in Jean Overton Fuller, *Swinburne* (1968), on Algernon Charles Swinburne

Thomas Carlyle meets A C Swinburne

All his life he loved attempting magnificent things in a slapdash way and, whatever others might think, he was seldom dissatisfied with the result.

DONALD CARSWELL (1882–1940) on J.S. Blackie, in *Brother Scots* (1927)

Joanna Baillie is now almost totally forgotten, even among feminist academics dredging the catalogues for third-rate women novelists . . . Her life story is a quaint one, interesting for being so dull.

> RUPERT CHRISTIANSEN, *Romantic Affinities* (1988),
> on the C19th tragedian Joanna Baillie

> . . . to conclude, they say in few words
> That Gilbert is not worth two cow turds,
> Because when he has crack't so crouse,
> His mountains just bring forth a mouse.

> SAMUEL COLVILLE or COLVIN, *Pindarique Ode on Bishop Burnet's
> 'Dialogues'*, c. 1689; Gilbert Burnet (1643–1715) became
> Bishop of Salisbury under William of Orange and was
> detested by both Presbyterians and Jacobites

The man's mind was not clean . . . he degraded and prostituted his intellect, and earned thereby the love and worship of a people whose distinguishing trait is fundamental lewdness . . . Put into decent English many of his most vaunted lays amount to nothing at all . . . His life as a whole would have discredited a dustman, much less a poet . . . a superincontinent yokel with a gift for metricism.

> T.W.H. CROSLAND, *The Unspeakable Scot* (1902),
> on Robert Burns (and his fellow countrymen)

. . . deplorable is the mildest epithet one can justly apply to it. Wordsworth writes somewhere of a person 'who would peep and botanise about his mother's grave'. This is exactly the feeling that a reading of *Margaret Ogilvy* gives you.

> T.W.H. CROSLAND, *The Unspeakable Scot*,
> on Sir J.M. Barrie's memoir of his mother

It is with publishers as with wives: one always wants someone else's.

NORMAN DOUGLAS (1868–1952)

Mr Coleridge was in bad health; – the particular reason is not given; but the careful reader will form his own conclusions . . . Upon the whole, we look upon this publication as one of the most notable pieces of impertinence of which the press has lately been guilty.

The *Edinburgh Review*, anonymous review of
Samuel Taylor Coleridge's *Kubla Khan* (1816)

On Waterloo's ensanguined plain
Lie tens of thousands of the slain;
But none, by sabre or by shot,
Fell half so flat as Walter Scott.

THOMAS, LORD ERSKINE (1750–1823),
on Sir Walter Scott's 'The Field of Waterloo'

It is a story of crofter life near Stonehaven; but it is question-able if the author, or authoress, is correct in the description of crofter girls' underclothing of that period.

Fife Herald book review of Lewis Grassic Gibbon's
Cloud Howe, quoted in L. Grassic Gibbon and
Hugh MacDiarmid, *Scottish Scene* (1934)

The bleatings of a sheep.

> JOHN FRASER, Professor of Celtic at Oxford University,
> on the translations from Gaelic of Kenneth Macleod (1871–1955),
> quoted in *The Memoirs of Lord Bannerman of Kildonan*

Mr Gunn is a brilliant novelist from Scotshire who chooses his home county as the scene of his tales . . . he is the greatest loss to itself that Scottish literature has suffered in this century.

> LEWIS GRASSIC GIBBON (James Leslie Mitchell, 1901–35),
> *Scottish Scene*

Welsh's market remains captive: the inarticulate 20-some-things, call-centre folk, cyberserfs, unsmug unmarrieds who infest [city centre] fun palaces. Welsh is to this lot what, in his happier days, Jeffrey Archer was to Mondeo Man: the jammy bastard who did well.

> CHRISTOPHER HARVIE (1944–) quoted by Senay Boztas,
> *Sunday Herald*, 23 January 2005, on Irvine Welsh

wee Maurice (most minuscule of makars)

> HAMISH HENDERSON (1920–2002), letter to Hugh MacDiarmid,
> 3 April 1949, on Maurice Lindsay

The final word on Burns must always be that he is the least rewarding of his country's major exports, neither so nourishing as porridge, or stimulating as whisky, nor so relaxing as golf.

> KENNETH HOPKINS, *English Poetry*, quoted in
> Hugh MacDiarmid, *Lucky Poet* (1943)

If you imagine a Scotch commercial traveller in a Scotch commercial hotel leaning on the bar and calling the barmaid Dearie, then you will know the keynote of Burns's verse.

> A.E. HOUSMAN (1859–1936), quoted in Jonathon Green,
> *Dictionary of Insulting Quotations* (1996)

Dr Donne's verses are like the Peace of God, for they pass all understanding.

> KING JAMES VI (1566–1625), attributed,
> on the poems of John Donne

This will never do!

> LORD JEFFREY (1773–1850), reviewing Wordsworth's
> 'The Excursion' in *The Edinburgh Review*, November 1814

Writers are too difficult.

> A member of the Glasgow Festivals Unit team, on why so few
> writers were involved in the city's 'Culture Year' (1990),
> quoted in James Kelman, *Some Recent Attacks* (1992)

Yuh wrote? A po-it? Micht ye no' juist as weel hae peed inti thuh wund?

> MAURICE LINDSAY (1918–) recalling the comment of an
> anonymous Glaswegian 'In a Glasgow Loo',
> from Robin Bell, *The Best of Scottish Poetry* (1989)

Does she, poor silly thing, pretend
The manners of our age to mend?
Mad as we are, we're wise enough
Still to despise sic paultry stuff.

JANET LITTLE (1759–1813),
'Given to a Lady Who Asked Me To Write a Poem'

. . . calm, settled, imperturbable drivelling idiocy . . . We will venture to make one small prophecy, that his bookseller will not a second time venture £50 on any thing he can write. It is a better and a wiser thing to be a starved apothecary than a starved poet; so back to the shop, Mr John, back to 'plasters, pills, and ointment boxes, etc'.

J.G. LOCKHART (1794–1854), in *Blackwood's Magazine*,
1818, on John Keats's 'Endymion'

James Boswell

Servile and impertinent, shallow and pedantic, a bigot and a sot, bloated with family pride, and eternally blustering about the dignity of a born gentleman, yet stooping to be a talebearer, and eavesdropper, a common butt in the taverns of London . . . Everything which another man would have hidden, everything the publication of which would have made another man hang himself, was matter of exaltation to his weak and diseased mind.

LORD MACAULAY (1800–59),
on James Boswell (1740–95)

> . . . high-falutin' nonsense,
> Spiritual masturbation of the worst sort.

> HUGH MACDIARMID (C.M. Grieve, 1892–1978), on the
> 'Celtic Twilight' works of Fiona Macleod
> (William Sharp, 1856–1905)

I remember well when Mr Lindsay first climbed on to the bandwagon of the Scottish Renaissance Movement. He came to see me about it. I had no difficulty whatever in appreciating that under his natty khaki shirt what may be described as his bosom was warming with the glowing ecstasy of a dog sighting a new and hitherto undreamed-of lamp-post.

> HUGH MACDIARMID (C.M. Grieve, 1892–1978),
> 'A Soldier's Farewell to Maurice Lindsay', in *National Weekly*
> (June 1952); Lindsay had criticised MacDiarmid's introduction to
> a Scottish concert at the Institute of Contemporary Arts, London

> Calf-fighter Campbell . . .
> there's an operation to do first
> – To remove the haemorrhoids you call your poems

> HUGH MACDIARMID (C.M. Grieve, 1892–1978),
> on Roy Campbell, the Spanish-dwelling Scoto-South African poet

> Campbell, they call him – 'crooked mouth' that is –
> But even Clan Campbell's records show no previous case
> Of such extreme distortion, of a mouth like this
> Slewed round to a man's bottom from his face
> And speaking with a voice not only banal
> But absolutely anal

> HUGH MACDIARMID (C.M. Grieve, 1892–1978),
> still on Roy Campbell

There was another old lady who knew and loved the songs of the bard William Ross. This particular morning she spent singing William Ross's songs behind closed doors. A pious neighbour overheard her beautiful singing . . . She came in later and said, 'Yours was the beautiful singing this morning. Surely it was the Psalms of David that you sang.'

'David, the excremental blackguard!' replied the other.

'What good was he compared to William Ross?'

CALUM MACLEAN, *The Highlands of Scotland* (1975)

He is writing a novel and his characters all want soaking in double strong disinfectant for a week.

RHEA MITCHELL, wife of Lewis Grassic Gibbon, in a letter of March 1927 about his first novel, *Stained Radiance*

Men of sorrow, and acquainted with Grieve.

EDWIN MUIR (1887–1959), on the Scottish writers of his time

Next to tartan and soldiers, poetry is the greatest curse of contemporary Scotland. It is the intellectuals' special form of dope, which they can indulge in with a good conscience while the crowds go mad up on the Castle esplanade.

TOM NAIRN (1932–), 'Festival of the Dead', in *New Statesman*, September 1967

For thee, James Boswell, may the hand of Fate
Arrest thy goose-quill and confine thy prate!
. . . To live in solitude, oh! be thy luck,
A chattering magpie on the Isle of Muck.

PETER PINDAR (John Wolcot, 1738–1819), *Bozzy and Piozzi*

Ne'er
Was flattery lost on poet's ear;
A simple race! they waste their toil
For the vain tribute of a smile.

SIR WALTER SCOTT (1771–1832), *The Lay of the Last Minstrel*

Alexander MacDonald schoolmaster of Ardnamurchan is an offence to all sober well-inclin'd persons as he wanders thro' the country composing Gaelic songs, stuffed with obscene language.

Society for the Propagation of Christian Knowledge,
Minutes for June 1745, referring to Alexander MacDonald
(the poet Alasdair MacMaighstir Maighstir)

She has dedicated her menopause to me.

MURIEL SPARK (1918–2006) on an American editor
who criticised her autobiography, *Curriculum Vitae*

Poor Henry is on the point of death, and his friends declare that I have killed him. I received the information as a compliment, and begged they would not do me so much honour.

GILBERT STUART (fl. C18th), who conducted a literary vendetta
against the historian Dr Henry, in a letter, 3 April 1775

As artists we situate ourselves at the level of man-at-crap.

ALEXANDER TROCCHI (1925–84), quoted in Andrew Murray Scott,
Alexander Trocchi: The Making of the Monster (1991)

It is not poetry. Here, most frequently, we have neither rhyme nor reason. We have the utterance of much that should never find expression in decent society . . . It sounds like Homer after he had swallowed his false teeth.

LAUCHLAN MACLEAN WATT, reviewing Hugh MacDiarmid's poem 'To Circumjack Cencrastus' (in which there is a mocking reference to himself)

Even without a book to promote, Fry would, in the interests of self-publicity, cheerfully announce his conversion to the flatness of the earth or testify to his encounters in an Edinburgh hostelry with little men from outer space.

BRIAN WILSON, *Scotland on Sunday*, 8 October 2006, on the historian Michael Fry

As a poet Scott cannot live . . . What he writes in the way of natural description is merely rhyming nonsense.

WILLIAM WORDSWORTH (1770–1850), in a conversation reported by Mrs Davy, 1844, on Sir Walter Scott

Beasts and birds

She had the fiercie and the fleuk,
The scheerloch and the wanton yeuk;
On ilka knee she had a breuk –
What ail'd the beast to dee?

PATRICK BIRNIE (fl. 1660), 'The Auld Man's Mear's Dead'

I turned a grey stone over: a hundred forkytails seethed from
under it like thoughts out of an evil mind.

GEORGE MACKAY BROWN (1921–96), 'Five Green Waves'

Ye ugly, creepin, blasted wonner,
Detested, shunn'd by saint and sinner,
How daur ye set your fit upon her –
Sae fine a lady?
Gae somewhere else, and seek your dinner
On some poor body.

ROBERT BURNS (1759–96), 'To a Louse'

A puddock sat by the lochan's brim,
An' he thocht there was never a puddock like him . . .
A heron was hungry, and needin' tae sup,
Sae he nabbit the puddock and gollupt him up;

Syne runkled his feathers: 'A peer thing,' quo' he,
But – puddocks is nae fat they eesed tae be.'

J.M. CAIE (1878–1949), 'The Puddock'

The confounded fleas of mischief and grief . . .
If I could round you all up and stow you in a barrel
And were I blessed with the means I'd send you to Adolf,
Mixed with body-hugging crablice and bugs from the rugs
I'd have it poured about his skull and he'd be locked in his
room.

ANGUS CAMPBELL (1903–82), 'The Fleas of Poland', from the Gaelic

I kicked an Edinbro dug-lover's dug.
Leastways, I tried; my timing was ower late,
It stopped whit it was daein on my gate
An skelpit aff to find some ither mug.

ROBERT GARIOCH (Robert Garioch Sutherland, 1909–81),
'Nemo Canem Impune Lacessit'

Of all forms of life, surely the most vile. The cleg was silent, the
colour of old horse manure, a sort of living ghost of evil.

NEIL M. GUNN (1891–1973), *Highland River*, on the cleg

Snails too lazy to build a shed.

GEORGE MACDONALD (1824–1905), *Little Boy Blue*, on slugs

That the dogs are lousy is not to be wondered at, since so many of the islanders themselves spend their entire lives in that unsavoury condition.

ALASDAIR ALPIN MACGREGOR, *The Western Isles* (1949)

A cat may look at a king –
Oh, fairly, that!
But a king can swack the head
Frae ony cat.

ALEXANDER SCOTT (1920–89), 'Cat and King'

Curses and imprecations

The curse of hell frae me sall ye bear,
Mither, mither;
The curse of hell frae me sall ye bear,
Sic counsels ye gave to me, O.

Anonymous, 'Edward'

'Humpback is the heir of MacLeod today, and as long as dry
straw will burn, many a hump and crook will there be in the
clan hereafter.'

Curse by an old woman of Hulin, Eigg, on a MacLeod war party,
c. 1600, from the Gaelic

Curse Thou his basket and his store,
Kail an' potatoes.

ROBERT BURNS (1759–96), 'Holy Willie's Prayer'

Curs'd be the man, the poorest wretch in life,
The crouching vassal to a tyrant wife!

ROBERT BURNS (1759–96), 'The Henpecked Husband'

O Fergusson! thy glorious parts
Ill suited law's dry, musty arts!
My curse upon your whunstane hearts,
Ye E'nbrugh gentry!
The tythe o' what ye waste at cartes
Wad stow'd his pantry!

> ROBERT BURNS (1759–96), 'Epistle To William Simson',
> on poet Robert Fergusson (1750–74)

First on the head of him who did this deed
My curse shall light, – on him and all his seed:
Without one spark of intellectual fire,
Be all the sons as senseless as the sire:
If one with wit the parent brood disgrace,
Believe him bastard of a brighter race.

> LORD BYRON (1788–1824), 'The Curse of Minerva',
> on Lord Elgin (1766–1841), remover of the
> Parthenon sculptures from Athens to London

Columba was one day in the strand of the small fry and he trampled on a beautiful little fair Flounder and hurt her tail. The poor little Flounder cried out as loud as she could:

> 'Thou Colum big and clumsy
> With the crooked crosswise feet
> Much didst thou to me of injust
> When thou trampled on my tail.'

Columba was angry at being taunted with having crooked feet and he said:

> 'If I am crooked-footed,
> Be thou crooked-mouthed.'
> And he left her that way.

> ALEXANDER CARMICHAEL (1832–1912), from *Carmina Gadelica*

I curse their head and all the hairs of their head, I curse their face, their eyes, their mouth, their nose, their tongue, their teeth, their shoulders, their backs and their heart . . . Before and behind, within and without. I curse them walking and I curse them riding. I curse them standing and I curse them sitting . . . I dissever and part them from the Kirk of God, and deliver them quick to the devill of Hell.

> ARCHBISHOP DUNBAR OF GLASGOW (fl. early C16th),
> curse against those who break the laws of the Church,
> quoted in George Blake, *Scottish Treasure Trove* (c. 1930)

I denounce, proclaimis and declaris all and sundry the committaris of the said saikles murthris, slauchteris, brinying, herirchippen, reiffs, thiftis and spulezies . . . and their counsalouris and defendouris of thair evil deeds generalie CURSIT, waryit aggregeite, and reaggregaite, with the GREIT CURSING . . . All the malesouns and waresouns that ever gat warldlie creature sen the begynnyng of the warlde to this hour mot licht upon thaim.

The maledictioun of God, that lichtit apon Lucifer and all his fallows, that strak them frae the hie hevin to the deep hell, mot licht apon thaim . . . And their candillis gangis frae your sicht, as mot their saulis gang frae the visage of God, and thair gude faim fra the warld, quhile thai forbeir thair oppin synnis foirsaid, and rise frae this terribill cursing, and mak satisfactioun and pennance.

ARCHBISHOP GAVIN DOUGLAS OF GLASGOW (fl. early C16th), curse on the Border Reivers, quoted in George MacDonald Fraser, *The Steel Bonnets* (1971)

'De'il colic the wame o' thee, thou false thief! Dost thou say mass at my lug?'

Saying attributed to JENNY GEDDES, Edinburgh stallkeeper, on the occasion of the first attempt to read from Archbishop Laud's Liturgy in St Giles Cathedral (as it then was), 23 July 1637

Son of a Scots manse though you were
I've taken the rare scunner against you,
You who thieve the golden hours of bairns,
You who bitch up the world's peoples
With crystal images, pitch-black lies,
You who have ended civilised conversation
And dished out licences to print banknotes,
May your soul shrink to the size of a midge
And never rest in a couthie kirkyard
But dart across a million wee screens
And be harassed by TV jingles for ever and ever,
For thine's the kingdom of the televisor,
You goddam bloody genius, John Logie Baird!

ROBERT GREACEN (1920–), 'Curse'

Fra heat of body I thee now deprive,
And to thy sickness sall be na recure,
Bot in dolour thy dayis to endure.
Thy crystal ene minglit with blude I mak;
Thy voice so clear unpleasand, hoir and hace;
Thy lusty lire ourspersed with spottis black,
And lumpis haw appearand in thy face.

ROBERT HENRYSON (c. 1425–c. 1500), the curse of leprosy
put on Cressida, from *The Testament of Cresseid*

That d—d Sir Walter Scott, that everybody makes such a work
about! . . . I wish I had him to ferry over Loch Lomond: I
should be after sinking the boat, if I drowned myself into the
bargain; for ever since he wrote his *Lady of the Lake*, as they call
it, everybody goes to see that filthy hole Loch Katrine, then
comes round by Luss, and I have had only two gentlemen to
guide all this blessed season.

Loch Lomond ferryman, after publication of Scott's
Lady of the Lake in 1810

Curse his new hoose, his business, his cigar,
His wireless set, and motor car,
Alsatian, gauntlet gloves, plus-fours and wife,
— A' thing included in his life;
And, abune a', his herty laughter,
And, if he has yin, his hereafter.

HUGH MACDIARMID (C.M. Grieve, 1892–1978),
'Thoughts On My Boss'

My malison light ilka day,
On them that drink and dinna pay.

ALLAN RAMSAY (1686–1758), 'Lucky Spence's Last Advice'

Nothing will do in this country that has common sense in it;
only cant, hypocrisy and superstition will flourish here. A curse
upon the country, and all the men, women and children of it.

GILBERT STUART (fl. C18th),
letter to a London friend, 17 June 1774

Fyvie, Fyvie, thou's ne'er thrive ye
As lang as in thee there's stanis three:
There's ane intil the highest tower,
There's ane intil the ladye's bower,
There's ane aneath the water yett,
And thir three stanis ye'se never get!

THOMAS THE RHYMER (fl. C14th),
'Curse Upon Fyvie Castle'

Ugie, Ugie by the sea,
Lordless shall thy landis be,
And underneath thy hearthstane,
The tod shall bring her bairnis hame.

THOMAS THE RHYMER (fl. C14th),
'Curse Upon the Earl Marischal's Castle'

High though his titles, proud his name,
Boundless his wealth as wish can claim, –
Despite those titles, power and pelf
The wretch, concentred all in self,
Living, shall forfeit fair renown,
And doubly dying shall go down
To the vile dust from whence he sprung,
Unwept, unhonoured and unsung.

SIR WALTER SCOTT (1771–1832),
The Lay of the Last Minstrel

May William, the son of George, be as a leafless splintered tree, rootless, branchless, sproutless. May there be no joy on his hearth, no wife, no brother, no son, no sounding harp or blazing wax.

JOHN ROY STUART (fl. C18th),
'Curse Upon the Duke of Cumberland',
from the Gaelic (after Culloden, 1746)

Fuck off, ya plukey-faced wee hing-oot.

IRVINE WELSH (1958–), *Trainspotting*

Doctors and medicine

Did he dee a natural death, or was the doctor sent for?

Annandale saying, quoted in Charles Rodgers,
Familiar Illustrations of Scottish Life (1866)

My curse upon your venom'd stang
That shoots my tortur'd gums alang,
And thro' my lug gies sic a twang
Wi' gnawing vengeance.

ROBERT BURNS (1759–96),
'Address to the Toothache'

I have been far too frequently threatened by lunatics in and out of prison to worry about this lot.

DR JAMES DEVON, force-feeder of suffragette prisoners,
in Leah Leneman, *A Guid Cause* (1991), on his critics

Whenever patients come to I,
I physics, bleeds and sweats 'em;
If after that they choose to die,
What's that to me? I letts 'em.

THOMAS, LORD ERSKINE (1750–1823),
'Epigram on Dr John Lettsom'

Doctors, like mini-cab drivers, are the other idiots to whom we entrust our lives.

JAMES KENNAWAY (1928–68), *The Kennaway Papers*

Most native-born doctors indulge in a bit of poaching, a favourite activity of peasantry. The urge to poach is in the blood.

ALASDAIR ALPIN MACGREGOR, *The Western Isles* (1949)

England and the English

It was an ancient conceit of the Scots to pretend that the English were born with tails. In one of the legends of William Wallace, his famous confrontation with the English soldiers in Lanark (1296) began when he protected a small boy who had put his fingers behind his back and waggled them like a tail at the angry pikemen.

> To save a maid St George a dragon slew,
> A brave exployt if all that's said is true,
> Some think there are no dragons; nay, 'tis said
> There was no George; pray God there was a maid.

Anonymous lines on England's patron saint, C18th,
in J. Maidment, *Book of Scottish Pasquils* (1866)

Why do we always get Julians and Timothys? Let's get some Wullies in charge.

Anonymous protest against the appointment of an Englishman as
Director of the National Galleries of Scotland, quoted in
A. Cran and J. Robertson, *Dictionary of Scottish Quotations* (1996)

He is an egregious dissembler and a great liar. Away with him, he is a greeting divil.

> ROBERT BLAIR (1593–1666), in Thomas McCrie,
> *The Life of Mr Robert Blair* (1848), on Oliver Cromwell

. . . when I humour any of them in an outrageous contempt of Scotland, I fairly own I treat them as children. And thus I have, at some moments, found myself obliged to treat even Dr Johnson.

> JAMES BOSWELL (1740–95), *Journal of a Tour to the Hebrides*

. . . for the most part the worst instructed, and the least knowing of their rank, I ever went amongst.

> GILBERT BURNET (1643–1715), *History of His Own Times*,
> on the English aristocracy

On that night: John Bull was as Haughty and Valiant, as a few months ago he was abject and cowardly, on the Black Wednesday when the Highlanders were at Derby.

> ALEXANDER CARLYLE (1722–1805), *Recollections*; he was in London
> when the news of Culloden was received in 1746

Thirty millions, mostly fools.

> THOMAS CARLYLE (1795–1881), when asked what the
> population of England was

Even a boiled egg tastes of mutton fat in England.

> NORMAN DOUGLAS (1868–1952), *Old Calabria*

The Englishman remains everlastingly adolescent.

NORMAN DOUGLAS (1868–1952), *Old Calabria*

> Let bragart England in disdain
> Ha'd ilka lingo, but her ain:
> Her ain, we wat, say what she can,
> Is like her true-born Englishman,
> A vile promiscuous mungrel seed
> O' Danish, Dutch an' Norman breed,
> An' prostituted since, to a'
> The jargons on this earthly ba'!

ALEXANDER GEDDES (1737–1802), *Epistle to the Society of Antiquaries*

An Englishman is a man who lives on an island in the North Sea governed by Scotsmen.

PHILIP GUEDALLA, *Supers and Supermen* (1920)

I don't like the English. One at a time, I don't mind them. I've loved some of them. It's their collective persona I can't warm to: the lumpen and louty, coarse, unsubtle, beady-eyed, beefy-bummed herd of England.

The truth is – and perhaps this is a little unworthy, a bit shameful – I find England and the English embarrassing. Fundamentally toe-curlingly embarrassing. And even though I look like one, sound like one, can imitate the social/mating behaviour of one, I'm not one. I always bridle with irritation when taken for an Englishman, and fill in those disembarkation cards by pedantically writing 'Scots' in the appropriate box.

A.A. GILL (1954–), *The Angry Island*

. . . if one will only read the anecdotes of village 'loonies' with which Scots literature abounds . . . he will find that the average Scots idiot was a creature of considerably more humour than the average Englishman.

J.A. HAMMERTON, *J.M. Barrie and His Books* (1900)

The Barbarians who inhabit the banks of the Thames.

DAVID HUME (1711–76), letter to Hugh Blair, April 1764

I hate London, and I do not think that either flattery or profit can ever make me love it.

JAMES HOGG (1770–1835), letter to his wife, January 1832

Sir, it is not so much to be lamented that Old England is lost, as that the Scotch have found it.

SAMUEL JOHNSON (1709–84), to James Boswell, 15 May 1776

Boswell was praising the English highly, and saying they were a fine, open people. 'Oh –' said Macpherson, 'an open people! their mouths, indeed, are open to gluttony to fill their belly, but I know of no other openness they have.'

JAMES MACPHERSON (1734–96),
quoted in Charles Rogers, *Boswelliana* (1874)

I am heartily tired of this Land of Indifference and Phlegm where the finer Sensations of the Soul are not felt, and Felicity is held to consist in stupefying Port and overgrown Buttocks of Beef, where Genius is lost, and Taste altogether extinguished.

TOBIAS SMOLLETT (1721–71), letter to Alexander Carlyle, March 1754

Entertainment and the media

The music for the occasion was provided by the pipe band of the Queen Victoria School and by the military band of the 2nd Battalion Gordon Highlanders. There was no wind to speak of.

Inadvertent insult from a Perthshire local paper

Once at the Edinburgh Festival, two very genteel elderly local ladies were present at a performance of Shakespeare's *Pericles*, which opened on a stage strewn with mirrored cushions and beaten brass tables. 'Where is it supposed to be?' whispered one. Said the other, reading from the programme, 'Egypt – a brothel in Alexandria.' Declared the first, 'Och, it's nothing like a brothel in Alexandria.'

From NIGEL REES, *The Guinness Book of Humorous Anecdotes* (1994)

When a piper of very moderate ability rose to perform at a concert on Skye, a member of the audience shouted, 'Sit down, ye damn fool!' Instantly the chairman was on his feet: 'Who called the piper a damn fool?' Back flashed the reply: 'Who called the damn fool a piper?'

From DAVID ROSS, *MacRory's Breeks: And Other Highland Humour* (2002)

I have never had to try to get my act across to a non-English speaking audience, except at the Glasgow Empire.

ARTHUR ASKEY (1900–82), English comedian

Another English artiste, a male impersonator making one of several farewell appearances, also met a hostile uproar as soon as she appeared.

But she had a gallant champion. A tall gent rose from his seat in the front row of the stalls and faced the howling mob. 'Aw, come on,' he appealed to them. 'Gi'e the poor auld coo a chance.'

This unexpected intervention brought a brief period of silence during which the lady artiste walked to the footlights and rebuked the noisy mob with the heartfelt words, 'Thank goodness there's ONE gentleman in the audience.'

STANLEY BAXTER, *Stanley Baxter's Bedside Book of Glasgow Humour* (1986)

Edmund Burt tells the story of a military officer who added a drummer to complement the piper of his Highland company: Now the contest between the drummer and the piper arose about the point of honour, and at length the contention grew exceedingly hot, which the captain having notice of, he called them both before him, and, in the end, decided the matter in favour of the drummer; whereupon the piper remonstrated very warmly. 'Achs wuds, sir,' says he, 'and shall a little rascal, that beats upon a sheepskin, tak the right haund of me, that am a musician?'

EDMUND BURT, *Letters from the North of Scotland* (1720–37)

Such a set of ugly creatures as the Chorus I never did see! I grew so sorry for them, reflecting perhaps that each had a life of her own; that perhaps 'somebody loved that pig'; that, if I had any tears in me at the moment, I would have cried for them all packed there like herrings in a barrel, into one mass of sound.

JANE WELSH CARLYLE (1801–66),
on a performance of Handel's *Messiah*

. . . they brought in a kind of accordion and my hostess (who was regarded locally as a great musician) began with the utmost gravity to play on it the most atrocious tunes.

FREDERIC CHOPIN (1810–49), on a visit to the Duchess of Hamilton, quoted in T. Ratcliffe Barnett, *Scottish Pilgrimage in the Land of Lost Content* (1949)

Jocky, whose manly high–boned cheeks to crown,
With freckles spotted, flamed the golden down,
With meikle art could on the bagpipes play
E'en from the rising to the setting day;
Sawney as long without remorse could bawl
Home's madrigals and ditties from Fingal.

CHARLES CHURCHILL (1731–64), *The Prophecy of Famine*

The show is just 40 minutes long but, frankly, I'd rather have spent the time having a cervical smear test: it would have been more fun.

KATE COPSTICK, on *Blondes Have More Fun*,
in *The Scotsman*, 4 August 2005

To an artiste, applause is like a banquet . . . Thanks for the cheese sandwich.

BILLY CONNOLLY (1942–), to a Glasgow audience

Last time I saw a mouth like yours, pal, Lester Piggott was sitting behind it.

BILLY CONNOLLY (1942–), quoted in D. Campbell,
Billy Connolly: The Authorised Version (1976), to a heckler

Braveheart is pure Australian shite. Unless William Wallace went about with Dulux on his fuckin' face, in pigtails and a kilt. And then there's Rob Roy, poncing about the heather talking about honour. He was a spy, a thief, a blackmailer – a cunt, basically.

BILLY CONNOLLY (1942–), interview with Bob Flynn
in *The Guardian*, April 1996

... journalism suits the Scots as it is a profession into which you can crawl without enquiry as to your qualifications, and because it is a profession in which the most middling talents will take you a long way.

T.W.H. CROSLAND, *The Unspeakable Scot* (1902)

Fair hellish.

DONALD DEWAR (1937–2000), first First Minister of Scotland, on some Edinburgh Festival Fringe shows, 1999

At the first performance of Douglas, when young Norval was busy giving out one of his rodomontading speeches, a canny Scot, who had been observed to grow more and more excited as the piece progressed, unable to contain his feelings, called out with evident pride, 'Whaur's yer Wully Shakespeare noo?'

JAMES C. DIBDIN, *Annals of the Edinburgh Stage* (1888), referring to the first performance of John Home's play, in Edinburgh, December 1756

The House of Terror.

KEN DODD (1927–), English comedian, BBC Radio, 8 June 1990, referring to the Glasgow Empire theatre

Williamson soon lost patience with a noisy group of young Americans in the audience at a performance of Macbeth. He got off his throne, walked down to the footlights, and calmly said, in iambic pentameters:

If you don't shut your mouths a friend of mine
Will pass among you with a baseball bat.

Whereupon he adjusted his crown and continued in complete silence.

> SHEILA HANCOCK, *Ramblings of an Actress* (1987),
> on the actor Nicol Williamson

It's all lies and trash anyway.

Arran ferryman, on seeing the daily newspapers fall into the water, quoted in Alastair Hetherington, *News, Newspapers and Television*

I have long ago learnt that the only true things in the newspapers are the advertisements.

> NORMAN LAMONT, quoted in *The Independent*, 3 December 1994

Pauper: I will not gif for all your play worth an sowis fart.

> SIR DAVID LINDSAY (c. 1486–1555), *Ane Satyre of The Thrie Estaitis*

How dare anyone discharge, and in the name of singing, the cacophony to be heard at the popular Gaelic concert?

> ALASDAIR ALPIN MACGREGOR, *The Western Isles* (1949)

How could they have mistaken the bagpipes for a musical instrument?

> JOHN MCILWRATH (d. 2007),
> Scottish-Canadian broadcaster

Of course, with the kind of people who call Mrs Kennedy-Fraser's travesties of Gaelic songs 'faithful reproductions of the spirit of the original' I have no dispute. They are harmless as long as ignorance and crassness are considered failings in criticism of poetry.

SORLEY MACLEAN (1911–96), *Criticism and Prose Writings*

He joined the *Daily Record* as Art Editor – a position, he recalls, which had extremely little to do with art, and almost nothing to do with editing.

MAGNUS MAGNUSSON AND OTHERS, *The Glorious Privilege* (1957), on Sir Alastair Dunnett

If fiddling is music, that's enough of it.

RODERICK MORISON (An Clàrsair Dall, the Blind Harper, c. 1655–c. 1714), on hearing a harp tune played on the fiddle, from the Gaelic

. . . that patchwork of blasphemy, absurdity, and gross obscenity, which the zeal of an early Reformer spawned under the captivating title of Ane Compendious Booke of Godlie and Spirituall Songs is neither comprehended under the description of song as we are now in quest of, nor do its miserable and profane parodies reflect any trace whatsoever of the stately ancient narrative ballad.

WILLIAM MOTHERWELL (1797–1835), Introduction to *Minstrelsy Ancient and Modern*, on the Wedderburn brothers' *Gude and Godlie Ballatis*

Put no faith in aught that bears the name of music while you are in Scotland . . . I was asked to a private concert; I suffered the infliction of several airs with exemplary patience.

AMÉDÉE PICHOT,
French consul in Edinburgh, 1822,
in Catherine and Donald Carswell,
The Scots Week-End (1936)

. . . the dank euphonies of the Glasgow Orpheus Choir

ALAN SHARP, 'A Dream of Perfection', in
I. Archer and T. Royle,
We'll Support You Evermore (1976)

I listen to Scottish dance music, as I am immune to it now, and it doesn't affect me.

IAIN CRICHTON SMITH (1928–98),
'Seordag's Interview with the BBC', in *Thoughts of Murdo*

bitch journalism

SIR DAVID STEEL (1938–),
former president of the
Scottish parliament,
September 1999

. . . to me the press is the mouth of a sewer, where lying is professed as from a university chair, and everything prurient, and ignoble, and essentially dull finds its abode and pulpit.

ROBERT LOUIS STEVENSON (1850–94), letter to Edmund Gosse

A good taxi-driver wasted.

A crack against himself by Edinburgh comedian Johnny Victory,
whose father ran a taxi business

Epitaphs

Epitaph composers often did not wait for the death of their subject, especially when the comment was a critical one. They wanted him, or her, to know in advance. It was a favourite form of epigrammatic character description, either in praise or disparagement.

Here lies a man beside a witch,
Who did oppress both poor and rich;
But whoe he is, or how she fares,
No man doth know, and als few cares.

Anonymous

Beneath this silent tomb is laid
A noisy antiquated maid,
Who from her cradle talked till death
And ne'er before was out of breath.

From Dalry, Ayrshire

On a cold pillow lies her head,
Yet it will rise again 'tis said;
So prudently reader how thy walk,
For if she rise again she'll talk.

From Biggar, Lanarkshire

Here lies Mary, the wife of John Ford
We hope her soul is gone to the Lord
But if for Hell she has changed this life
She had better be there than be John Ford's wife.

From Potterhill, Paisley, Renfrewshire

Here lies my wife
A slattern and shrew
If I said I regretted it
I should lie too.

From Devonside, Clackmannan

When Orpheus play'd he mov'd Old Nick,
But when you played you made us sick.

On a fiddler; said to have been seen in the Mearns

Here lies Tam Reid
Who was chokit to deid
Wi' takin a feed
O' butter and breid
Wi' owre muckle speed,
When he had nae need,
But just for greed.

Said to have been seen at Cromarty, Ross & Cromarty

Here lies an old woman wrapt in her linen,
Mother to James and Thomas Binnen;
Who for want of a coffin was buried in a girnal,
The earth got the shell, and the De'il got the kernel.

Said to have been seen at Deer, Aberdeenshire

This martyr was by Peter Ingles shot
By birth a Tiger rather than a Scot
Who that his monstrous extract might be seen
Cut off my head and kicked it o'er the Green
Thus was the head which was to wear a crown
A football made by a profane dragoon.

On a Covenanter from Fenwick, Ayrshire, 1685

My wife lies here, conveniently,
She is at rest, and so am I.

Said to have been transcribed in a Perthshire graveyard

John Adams lies here o' this parish
A carrier who carried his ale with relish.
He carried so much, he carried so fast,
He could carry no more, so was carried at last:
For the liquor he drank being too much for one
He could carry off, so he's now carrion.

On a Fife carrier, C18th

Here continueth to stink
The memory of the Duke of Cumberland
Who with unparalleled barbarity,
And inflexible hardness of heart,
In spite of all motives to lenity
That policy or humanity could suggest,
Endeavoured to ruin Scotland
By all the ways a Tyrant could invent.

> Anonymous Jacobite 'epitaph' for
> the Duke of Cumberland,
> written after the battle
> of Culloden, 1746

Here, Reader, turn your weeping eyes,
My fate a useful moral teaches;
The hole in which my body lies
Would not contain one half my speeches.

> Lines composed on himself
> by LORD BROUGHAM, sometime
> lord chancellor (1778–1868)

Here lyes beneath thir laid-stanes
The carcase of George Glaid-stanes
Wherever be his other half,
Loe here, yee's have his Epitaph.

> Anonymous epitaph for George Gladstanes,
> Archbishop of St Andrews (d. 1615);
> Row's *History of the Kirk* noted
> 'He lived a filthie belliegod; he died
> of a filthie and loathsome disease'

Gow and time are even now;
Gow beat time; now Time beats Gow.

On Neil Gow, violinist (d. 1807)

Here lies Mass Andrew Gray,
Of whom no muckle good can I say!
He was ne Quaker, for he had no spirit;
He was ne papist, for he had no merit;
He was ne Turk, for he drank muckle wine;
He was ne Jew, for he eat muckle swine;
Full forty years he preached and le'ed
For which God doomed him when he de'ed.

On the Rev. Andrew Gray, Glasgow

Heir layes a lord quho quhill he stood
Had matchless been had he been . . .;
This Epitaph's a Sylable short,
And ye may add a Sylable to it,
But quhat yat Sylable doeth importe,
My defunct lord could never doe it.

On Thomas Hamilton,
Earl of Haddington (d. 1637)

Within this circular idea
Call'd vulgarly a tomb.
The ideas and impressions lie
That constituted Hume.

Mock epitaph for the sceptical
philosopher David Hume (d. 1776),
published in *A Scotch Haggis* (c. 1820)

Here continueth to rot
The body of Francis Charteris,
Who, with an Inflexible Constancy and
Inimitable Uniformity of Life
Persisted
In spite of Age and Infirmities
In the practice of Every Human Vice,
Excepting Prodigality and Hypocrisy:
His insatiable Avarice exempted him from the first,
His matchless Impudence from the second.

JOHN ARBUTHNOT (1667–1735), composed for a contemporary

Here lies Boghead among the dead,
In hopes to get salvation;
But if such as he in Heav'n may be,
Then welcome – hail! damnation.

ROBERT BURNS (1759–96), on James Grieve,
Laird of Boghead, Tarbolton

Below thir stanes lie Jamie's banes;
O Death, it's my opinion,
Thou ne'er took such a bleth'rin bitch
Into thy dark dominion.

ROBERT BURNS (1759–96), 'On a Noisy Polemic'
(James Humphrey, a mason of Mauchline)

As father Adam first was fool'd
(A case that's still too common),
Here lies a man a woman ruled –
The devil ruled the woman.

ROBERT BURNS (1759–96), 'On a Henpecked Squire'

Lament him, Mauchline husbands a',
He aften did assist ye;
For had ye staid hale weeks awa,
Your wives they ne'er had missed ye.
Ye Mauchline bairns, as on ye press
To school in bands thegither,
O tread you lightly on his grass, –
Perhaps he was your father!

ROBERT BURNS (1759–96), 'On a Wag in Mauchline'
(the poet's friend James Smith)

Whoe'er thou art, O reader, know
That Death has murder'd Johnie;
An' here his body lies fu' low;
For saul he ne'er had ony.

ROBERT BURNS (1759–96), 'On "Wee Johnie"'
(generally taken to be John Wilson, printer of the first edition of
Burns's poems, at Kilmarnock)

Sic a reptile was Wat, a miscreant slave,
That the worms even damned him when laid in his grave;
'In his flesh there's a famine,' a starved reptile cries,
'And his heart is rank poison,' another replies.

ROBERT BURNS (1759–96), 'On Mr Walter Riddell'
(dropped by the Riddell family, Burns took a poet's vengeance)

Here lies with Death auld Grizel Grim
Lincluden's ugly witch
O Death, how horrid is thy taste
To lie with such a bitch.

ROBERT BURNS (1759–96), 'On Grizel Grim'

Here lies in earth a root of Hell,
Set by the Deil's ain dibble;
This worthless body damn'd himsel,
To save the Lord the trouble.

> ROBERT BURNS (1759–96),
> 'On D.C., a suicide'

Here lies John Bushby – honest man!
Cheat him, Devil – if you can.

> ROBERT BURNS (1759–96),
> 'On John Bushby, Tinwald Downs'

'Stop thief!' dame Nature call'd to Death,
As Willy drew his latest breath;
'How shall I make a fool again,
My choicest morsel thou hast ta'en.'

> ROBERT BURNS (1759–96),
> 'On William Graham of Mossknowe'

Here lies 'mang ither useless matters,
A. Manson wi' his endless clatters.

> ROBERT BURNS (1759–96),
> 'On an Innkeeper in Tarbolton',
> Andrew Manson (clatters: gossiping)

Here lies a mock-marquis, whose titles were shamm'd,
If he ever rise – it will be to be damn'd.

> ROBERT BURNS (1759–96),
> 'For Mr Marquis, a Dumfries tavern-keeper,
> who asked for an epitaph'

In se'enteen hunder'n forty-nine,
The deil gat stuff to make a swine,
An' coost it in a corner;
But wilily he changed his plan,
An' shaped it something like a man,
An' ca'd it Andrew Turner.

ROBERT BURNS (1759–96), 'On *Andrew Turner*'

Here lies, of sense bereft –
But sense he never had.
Here lies, by feeling left –
But that is just as bad.
Here lies, reduced to dirt –
That's what he always was.

GEORGE OUTRAM (1805–56), 'Here Lies'

Family life

Ye've gey little to complain o', man. Ye should be thankful ye're no married tae her.

LORD BRAXFIELD (1722–99), to his butler,
who complained about Lady Braxfield's manner

'Ye damned stupid bitch . . . I beg your pardon, mem. I took ye for my wife.'

LORD BRAXFIELD (1722–99), to his partner at whist

Yestreen I had a pint o' wine,
A place where body saw na;
Yestreen lay on this breast o' mine,
The gowden locks of Anna . . .
The Kirk and State may join and tell,
To do sic things I mauna:
The Kirk and State may gae to hell,
And I'll gae to my Anna.

ROBERT BURNS (1759–96), 'The Gowden Locks of Anna';
Anna Park, a Dumfries barmaid, was mother to his last child

She has an e'e, she has but ane,
The cat has twa the very colour;
Five rusty teeth, forbye a stump,
A clapper tongue wad deave a miller;

59

A whiskin beard about her mou',
Her nose and chin they threaten ither;
Sic a wife as Willie had,
I wad na gie a button for her.

ROBERT BURNS (1759–96), 'Willie Wastle'

She tauld thee weel thou wast a skellum,
A blethering, blustering, drunken blellum

ROBERT BURNS (1759–96), *Tam o' Shanter*

. . . a Highland woman, who, begging a charity of a Lowland laird's lady, was asked several questions, and, among the rest, how many husbands she had had? To which she answered, three. And being further questioned, if her husbands had been kind to her, she said the first two were honest men, and very careful of their family, for they both 'died for the law' – that is, were hanged for theft. 'Well, but as to the last?' 'Hout!' says she, 'a fulthy peast! He dy'd at hame, lik an auld dug, on a puckle o' strae.'

EDMUND BURT (c. 1695–1755),
Letters from a Gentleman in the North of Scotland

I abominate the sight of them so much that I have always had the greatest respect for the character of Herod.

LORD BYRON (1788–1824), letter to Augusta Leigh,
30 August 1811, on children

Ay, when that caribald carl wald climb on my wame,
                    [*lecherous fellow, belly*]
Then am I dangerus and dain and dour of my will; [*quiet*]
Yet let I never that larbar my leggis gae between,
To fyle my flesh, na fumyll me, without a fee great. [*tumble*]

WILLIAM DUNBAR (c. 1460–c. 1520), *The Tretis of the Twa Mariit Wemen and the Wedo*

Millions o' women bring forth in pain millions o' bairns that arenae worth haein'.

Proverbial saying quoted in Bill Duncan, *The Wee Book of Calvinism*, 2004

Sometimes yew felt like dropping dead, just to escape the company.

JAMES KELMAN (1946–), *The Good Times*

Wi' every effort to be fair
And no undue antagonism
I canna but say that my sweetheart's mither
Is a moolie besom, a moolie besom,
Naething but a moolie besom!

HUGH MACDIARMID (1892–1978), 'A Moolie Besom'

Hugh MacDiarmid

The indignant husband explained the reason for his wrath: had he not good cause for stabbing a wife who was unfaithful to him? If he expected the cummers of Aberlady to sympathise, and denounce the erring woman, he got a drop, for one of them stepped forward and retorted, 'Losh, if that be the trouble, you might as well stick us a' in Aberlady.'

AUGUSTUS MUIR, *Heather Track and High Road* (1944)

You're like every other boy that was born, picked up from the Bass Rock you were, that's where your father got you, didn't you know? Why didn't he go to the May Island, the silly kipper that he was, and bring us back a nice wee lassie instead of you, you nasty little brat.

CHRISTOPHER RUSH,
A Twelvemonth and a Day (1985)

Fashion and clothing

A' our town needlers are growing sae grand,
That strangers would tak' them for ladies o' land,
With their fine silken gowns and their black satin bags,
But mark what's below them is naething but rags.

Anonymous, *The Dandies of Deception*, c. 1830,
on the town-girls of Scotland

The common habit of the ordinary Highlanders is far from
being acceptable to the eye . . . this dress is called the quelt; and
for the most part, they wear the petticoat so very short, that in
a windy day, going up a hill, or stooping, the indecency of it is
plainly discovered.

EDMUND BURT (c. 1695–1755),
Letters from a Gentleman in the North of Scotland

. . . my fellow-passenger in the railway, took it into his head to smile very visibly when I laid off my white broadbrim, and suddenly produced out of my pocket my grey Glengarry . . . I looked straight into his smiling face and eyes, with a look which I suppose enquired of him, 'Miserable ninth part of the fraction of a tailor, art thou sure thou hast a right to smile at me?' The smile instantly died into another expression of emotion.

THOMAS CARLYLE (1795–1881), letter to his wife

The garb of old Gaul is no doubt very fetching from the point of view of the weak-minded, but of its effeminacy there can be no doubt. Really it is a costume for small and pretty boys who are too young to be breeched.

T.W.H. CROSLAND, *The Unspeakable Scot* (1902)

The Hielan' man he wears the kilt, even when it's snowin'; He kens na where the wind comes frae, but he kens fine where it's goin'.

JOE GORDON, 'The Hielan' Chorus'

In terms of dress sense, little thought is given to style outside Glasgow.

JAMIE GRANT, *The Cultureshock Guide to Scotland*, 2006

We Scots put up with lots of questions. 'What do you wear under your kilt?' is a common one. Only last week I had to listen while an Englishman explained that no-one in Scotland wanted to pay for underpants and that kilts were a handy excuse not to do so.

I explained they were wrong, and that in fact the English had stolen all our underpants. But that we still had all the washing powder.

BRIAN HENNIGAN, *The Scotsman*, 10 August 2005

Cursed be the king who stretched our stockings;
down in the dust may his face be found.

JOHN MACCODRUM (c. 1693–1779), 'Oran Mu'n Eideadh
Ghaidealach' (Song of the Highland Dress),
on the banning of the kilt and tartan, 1746

O, the pale breeches
cast a gloom on us this year . . .
. . . had we all been loyal
to the king who appealed to us,
we had not been seen till Doomsday
submitting to this garment.

DUNCAN BÀN MACINTYRE (1724–1812),
'Oran Dho 'N Brioghais' (Song of the Trousers)

I'm not to blame – the tailor is,
A blundering fool was he,
That buttons put behind my back,
Where I had not eyes to see.

ROB DONN MACKAY (c. 1714–1778), from the Gaelic,
verse written at age four or five, objecting to the
frock in which small boys used to be clad until
old enough to assume kilt or breeches

Wi' shanks like that ye'd better hae stuck to breeks!

CHARLES MURRAY (1864–1941), *Ay, Fegs*,
call from the crowd to a soldier in a kilt

This tartan obsession – prior to Walter Scott the average clan gathering looked like a parade of tattie bags.

W. GORDON SMITH, *Mr Jock* (1987)

Fictional insults

'My lady, there are few more impressive sights than a Scotsman on the make.'

SIR J.M. BARRIE (1860–1937), *What Every Woman Knows*

'You've forgotten the grandest moral attribute of a Scotsman, Maggie, that he'll do nothing which might damage his career.'

SIR J.M. BARRIE (1860–1937), *What Every Woman Knows*

Oh the gladness of her gladness when she's glad,
And the sadness of her sadness when she's sad;
But the gladness of her gladness,
And the sadness of her sadness
Are as nothing . . .
To the badness of her badness when she's bad.

SIR J.M. BARRIE (1860–1937), 'Rosalind'

London! Pompous Ignorance sits enthroned there and welcomes Pretentious Mediocrity with flattery and gifts . . . she entraps great men and sucks their blood.

J.M. BRIDIE (Osborne Henry Mavor, 1888–1951), *The Anatomist*

67

When the Deacon was not afraid of a man he stabbed him straight; when he was afraid of him he stabbed him on the sly.

> GEORGE DOUGLAS (George Douglas Brown, 1869–1902)
> *The House With the Green Shutters*

'Jock Goudie' – an envious bodie will pucker as if he had never heard the name – 'Jock Goudie? Wha's he for a Goudie? Oh ay, let me see now. He's a brother o' – eh,' (tittit-titting on his brow) – oh, just a brother o' Drucken Will Goudie o' Auchterwheeze! Oo-oh, I ken him fine. His grannie keepit a sweetieshop in Strathbungo.'

> GEORGE DOUGLAS (George Douglas Brown, 1869–1902),
> *The House with the Green Shutters*

He dois as dotit dog that damys on all bussis, [*urinates, bushes*] And liftis his leg apone loft, thoght he nocht list pische. [*does not want to*]

> WILLIAM DUNBAR (c. 1460–c. 1520),
> *The Tretis of the Twa Marriit Wemen and the Wedow*

'Ye're nut on, laddie. Ye're on tae nothin' . . . A gutless wonder like you, that hasn't got the gumption of a louse.'

> ARCHIE HIND (1928–), *The Dear Green Place*

'You are, sir, a presumptuous self-conceited pedagogue . . . a mildew, a canker-worm in the bosom of the Reformed Church.

> JAMES HOGG (1770–1835), *The Private Memoirs and Confessions of a Justified Sinner*

'What a wonderful boy he is,' said my mother.

'I'm feared he turn out to be a conceited gowk,' said old Barnet, the minister's man.

JAMES HOGG (1770–1835), *The Private Memoirs and Confessions of a Justified Sinner*

There was a smug, trim, smooth little minister, making three hundred a year pimping for a God in whom his heart was too small to believe.

ERIC LINKLATER (1899–1974), *Magnus Merriman*

She looks like a million dollars, but she only knows a hundred and twenty words and she's only got two ideas in her head.

ERIC LINKLATER (1899–1974), *Juan in America*

Ya knee-crept, Jesus-crept, swatchin' little fucker, ah'll cut the bliddy scrotum aff ye! Ah'll knacker and gut ye, ah'll eviscerate ye! Ya hure-spun, bastrified, conscrapulated young prick, ah'll do twenty years for mincin' you . . . ya parish-eyed, perishin' bastart.

RODDY MACMILLAN, *The Bevellers* (1973)

You think he's twistit. Ye want tae have seen his oul' man.

RODDY MACMILLAN, *The Bevellers* (1973)

Waldo is one of those people who would be enormously improved by death.

SAKI (H.H. Munro, 1870–1916), *Beasts and Super-Beasts*

The wee man's gotten his parritch at last.

> Dramatised version of Sir Walter Scott's *Rob Roy*,
> observation by the Dougal Cratur on the death of Rashleigh

Wha wadna be in love
Wi' bonnie Maggie Lauder?
A piper met her gaun to Fife,
And spier'd what was't they ca'd her: [*asked*]
Richt scornfully she answered him,
Begone, you hallanshaker! [*disturber of the peace*]
Jog on your gate, you bladderskate, [*Go on your way*]
My name is Maggie Lauder.

> FRANCIS SEMPILL (c. 1616–c. 1685), 'Maggie Lauder'

There ye gang, ye daft
And doitit dotterel, ye saft
Crazed outland skalrag saul.

> SYDNEY GOODSIR SMITH (1915–75),
> *The Grace of God and the Meths Drinker*

I have been the means, under God, of hanging a great number,
but never just such a disjaskit rascal as yourself.

> ROBERT LOUIS STEVENSON (1850–1894), *Weir of Hermiston*

Robert Louis Stevenson

I dinna like McFarlane, I'm safe enough tae state.
His lug wad cast a shadow ower a sax-fit gate.
He's saft as ony goblin and sliddery as a skate,
McFarlane o' the Sprots o' Burnieboozie.

G. Bruce Thomson, 'McFarlane o' the Sprots o' Burnieboozie'

He was built like a Toby-jug and his face had the complexion
and texture of poisoned veal.

Jeff Torrington (1935–), *The Last Shift*

Flyting

A flyting was a public dialogue between two poets in which each set out to brag about his own abilities and decry those of his rival. These combinations of poetical skill, scholarly learning, and crude abusiveness are a distinctively Scottish form of confrontational art. In origin they may be a warped relic of the formal disputations that were common in medieval scholarship. Perhaps they also owe something to the tradition of the Gaelic satirists and the power of their words to raise boils on a victim's skin or even to cause his death. The high point of flyting was in the late fifteenth and early sixteenth centuries when it was an entertainment at the courts of James IV and James V. The winner of the verbal joust would be rewarded with the royal favour and royal gold: the loser would have his status reduced – at least until next time. William Dunbar was a keen practitioner of the art of flyting, with Walter Kennedy among his opponents. King James V was even willing to engage in the game himself. Flyting always made full use of the Scots language's alliterative expressiveness.

Says Kennedy:

> Ignorant elf, aip, owll irregular,
> Skaldit skaitbird, and common shamelar;
> Wan-fukkit funling, that natour maid ane yrle,
>> [*nature, dwarf*]
> Baith Iohine the Ros and thow sall squeill and
> skirle,
> And evir I heir ocht of your making mair.
>> [*writing more verses*]

Says Dunbar, picking on Kennedy's provincial Ayrshire Gaelic background:

> Iersche brybour bard, vyle beggar with thy brattis
> Cuntbittin crawdoun Kennedy, coward of kynd . . .
> They trechour tung has tane ane heland strynd –
> Ane lawland ers wald make a bettir noyis.
> Deulbere, thy spere of were, but feir, thou yclde,
> Hangit, mangit, eddir-stangit, strynde stultorum,
> To me, maist hie Kenydic, and flec the felde,
> Pickit, wickit, convickit Lamp Lollardorum,
> Defamyt, blamyt, schamyt, Primas Paganorum.
> Out! Out! I schout, apon that snowt that snevillis.
> Tale tellare, rebellare, induellar wyth the deviliis,
> Spynk, sink with stink ad Tertara Termagorum.

In other words, 'Dunbar, you yield your spear of war, mere coward, hanged, addle-brained, adder-bitten, of the race of idiots, to me, most high Kennedy, and run from battle. Miserly, evil, damned Lamp of the Lollards, exposed, blamed, shamed, Chief among Pagans. Out, I shout, upon that snivelling snout. Tale-teller, rebel, dweller with devils. Sink, stinking dwarf, to the infernal regions of the Moorish devils.'

Two other flyting duellists were Alexander Montgomerie
(c. 1545–1611) and Patrick Hume of Polwarth (c. 1550–c. 1620).
Says Montgomerie:

> Polwart, ye peip like a Mouse among Thornes,
> No Cunning ye keip; Polwart, ye peip,
> Ye luik lyk a Sheip and ye had twa Hornes . . .
> Bewar what thou speikes, little Foul-earthe Tade, [*toad*]
> With thy Canigait Breeks, bewar what thou speiks,
> [*Canongate breeches*]
> Or ther sall be wat Chieks for the last that thou made . . .
> [*tears shed, composed*]
> And we mell thou sall yell, little cultron cuist.
> [*If we fight, knocked-down rascal*]

Says Polwarth:

> The ragged Roundels, raveand Royt, [*babbling rascal*]
> Some short, some lang, some out of Lyne,
> With scabrons Colours, fulsome Floyt,
> Proceedand from a Pynt of wine,
> Which haults for want of Feet like mine, [*limps, poetic metre*]
> Yet Fool thou thought no Shame to write 'm
> At Mens Commands that lacks Engine, [*intelligence*]
> Which doited Dyvours gart thee dite them.
> [*stupid layabouts, write*]
> Kaily lippis, kis my hippis, in grippis thou's behint . . .
> [*cabbagey*]
> Jock Blunt, thrawin frunt, kis the cunt of ane kow.
> Purs-peiller, hen steiller, cat keiller, now I know thee.
> [*skinflint*]

Polwarth especially could get carried away, threatening to
'drite [*shit*] in thy Gob' and ending in a catalogue of abuse in
which 'frog-fucker' is among the tamer insults hurled.

King James V wrote a flyting against Sir David Lindsay, poet and member of the court circle. His effort has not been preserved, but Lindsay responded with no holds barred, centring his approach on the monarch's penchant for lechery:

> . . . lyke ane boisteous bull, ye run and ryde
> Ryatouslie lyke ane rubiatoure
> Ay fukkand lyke ane furious fornicatour.

Sir David Lindsay (c. 1490–55),
'Answer to the King's Flyting'

Food, drink and hospitality

'Jock!' cried a farmer's wife to the cowherd, 'come awa' in to your parritch, or the flees 'll be droonin' themsel's in your milk bowl.'

'Nae fear o' that,' replied Jock. 'They could wade through it.'

'Ye rogue,' she cried, 'd'ye mean to say I dinna give ye eneuch milk?'

'Oh, aye,' said Jock, 'There's eneuch milk, for all the parritch that's in it.'

Traditional

'It's ten years old, you know,' said the lady of the house, pouring out some whisky for the plumber who had mended a burst pipe.

'Aye,' he said, looking at the only part-filled glass. 'And small for its age.'

Traditional

'I see you keep a bee.'

> *Xenophobe's Guide to the Scots* (1999), bed-and-breakfast
> visitor to landlady upon looking at the minuscule
> honey pot on the breakfast table

Our obliging landlady would, when requested, bring us a
pennyworth of soup, called kale, for our dinner, instead of
herring; and, if we had a little cause to remark on the want of
cleanliness in the dish, or the contents, she jocosely replied: 'It
tak's a deal o' dirt to poison sogers.'

> JAMES ANTON, *Retrospect of a Military Life* (1841)

'Tell me, have you eaten that, or are
you going to?'

> SIR J.M. BARRIE to Bernard Shaw,
> in C. Fadiman,
> *The Little Brown Book of Anecdotes* (1985),
> upon looking at Shaw's vegetarian meal

Is there that owre his french ragout,
Or olio wad stow a sow,
Or fricassé wad mak her spew
Wi' perfect sconner,
Looks down wi' sneering, scornfu' view
On sic a dinner?
Poor devil! See him owre his trash,
As feckless as a wither'd rash,
His spindle shank, a guid whip-lash,
His nieve a nit:
Thro' bloody flood or field to dash,
O how unfit!

> ROBERT BURNS (1759–96), 'Address to a Haggis'

The cook was too filthy an object to be described; only another English gentleman whispered me and said, he believed, if the fellow was to be thrown against the wall, he would stick to it.

EDMUND BURT (c. 1695–1755), *Letters from a Gentleman in the North of Scotland*, on the cook of an Edinburgh eating house

So that's the wey o' it! Yuletide's comin'.
Haverin' hypocrites, hear them talk:
Peace and good-will to men and women,
But thraw the neck o' the bubbly-jock.

W.D. COCKER (1882–1970), *The Bubbly-Jock*

. . . the potato, the grossly overrated potato, that marvel of insipidity

NORMAN DOUGLAS (1868–1952), *Together*

I don't think we have a cuisine to speak of.

ANDREW FAIRLIE, Scottish Chef of the Year, 2002

For rabbits young and for rabbits old,
For rabbits hot and for rabbits cold,
For rabbits tender and for rabbits tough,
Our thanks we render – but we've had enough.

ROBERT FERGUSSON (1750–74), 'Impromptu at St Salvator's College Hall, St Andrews', prompted by too much rabbit in the students' diet

'It's an awful thing the drink!' exclaimed a clergyman, when the barber, who was visibly affected, had drawn blood from his face for the third time.

'Aye,' replied the tonsorial artist, with a wicked leer in his eye, 'It mak's the skin tender.'

ROBERT FORD, *Thistledown* (1901)

Soon after his return from Scotland to London, a Scotch lady resident in the capital invited Dr Johnson to dinner, and in compliment to her distinguished guest ordered a dish of hotch-potch. When the great man had tasted it, she asked him if it was good, to which he replied with his usual gruffness, 'Very good for hogs, I believe.'

'Then, pray,' said the lady, 'let me help you to a little more.'

ROBERT FORD, *Thistledown* (1901)

After the bottle had circulated a few times, and the spirits of the assembly had begun to rise, General S——, an English trooper of fame, and a reckless bon vivant, arose and said, 'Gentleman, when I am in my cups, and the generous wine begins to warm my blood, I have an absurd custom of railing against the Scotch. Knowing my weakness, I hope no member of the company will take it amiss.'

He sat down, and a Highland chief, Sir Robert Bleakie, of Blair Atholl . . . quietly arose in his place, and with the utmost simplicity and good-nature, remarked, 'Gentlemen, when I am in my cups, and the generous wine begins to warm my blood, if I hear a man rail against the Scotch, I have an absurd custom of kicking him at once out of the company. Knowing my weakness, I hope no gentleman will take it amiss.'

It need scarcely be added that General S—— did not on that occasion suffer himself to follow his usual custom.

ROBERT FORD, *Thistledown* (1901),
on a London dinner party in the 1600s

. . . unquestionably the worst country in Europe to eat out in – or the worst country that didn't once have a communist dictator . . . It was the sight of Scots couples eating stinky detritus with concentrated gusto, as if just having someone else do the washing-up was worth the outing, that was so depressing. Outside the central belt and half a dozen heritage hotels, food is a sickly disaster for the Scots. They die younger than anyone else, not just because of the cholesterol, but because, in the end, they can't face another dinner.

A.A. GILL (1954–), *The Times*, 24 September 2006

Scotland has an uneviable reputation for serving up some of the most unhealthy, unappetising fare you can find under the guise of 'food'. You know the sort of thing: deep fried cholesterol with a side order of lard.

BEN JUDGE, *The Scotsman*, 25 February 2005

Having been to Oxford for a matinee, I duly arrived [at a dinner], dined, chatted and then rose to go around eleven.

'Thank you, Rachel, for a lovely dinner,' said my host to my wife.

'What do you mean?' I inquired.

'I brought it over from home,' Rachel explained, 'as their cook was off.'

'In that case,' I said, 'I am at liberty to say that the fish was the most disgusting thing I have ever eaten.'

'That was the only dish I provided,' said my host.

From ROBERT MORLEY, *A Book of Bricks*,
quoting playwright William Douglas-Home

Both in a river and in a dish
I hate that ubiquitous blasted fish.

ARNOLD SILCOCK, *Verse and Worse* (1952), 'Ode to a Salmon',
attributed to 'A Commander RN, in collaboration with
Flight Lieutenant James McGregor, RAF'

'That's the thing that angers me aboot an egg,' continued the
Captain. 'It never makes ye glad to see it on the table; ye know
at once the thing's a mere put-by because your wife or Jum
could not be bothered makin' something tasty.' 'We'll hae to
get the hens to put their heids together and invent a new kind
o' fancy egg for sailors,' said Sunny Jim.

NEIL MUNRO (1864–1930), *The Vital Spark*

The Frenchman offended the old Scotch peeress by some
highly disparaging remarks on Scottish dishes . . . all she would
answer was, 'Weel, weel, some fowk like parritch, and some
fowk like paddocks.'

DEAN E.B. RAMSAY (1793–1872),
Reminiscences of Scottish Life and Character

I'm horrified . . . after reading a press release from a hotel in
Scotland that went public in announcing the fact that they're
doing a deep-fried sandwich full of Nutella. I mean, Christ!
Seventy-five per cent of my staff are French. They look at me
like I'm some sort of twat that my Scottish brothers are
launching two slices of bread with a fucking inch of Nutella
between them, battered and deep fat fried. Now what the fuck
is this country coming to? What are we doing to ourselves?
That has to be abolished. Here we are, progressing tenfold,
buying the right bread, real croissants, we're making fresh
muesli and we understand what a great cup of coffee is. And

then some idiot brings out a deep-fried chocolate sandwich. I want to find the bastard that put that idea together. I've got the most amazing charcoal grill in my new kitchen. I'm going to sit his butt on it and criss-cross my name on his bloody arse cheeks to remind him. Every time he wakes up in the morning he can gawp at his arse. Is he fucking stupid? When these things hit France, the French just have a field day laughing at us. So I'm looking for that scumbag. I'm going to fucking grill his arse. Brand him with a hot iron like a little calf or a lamb. I'm going to put Ramsayfied on his butt, so every time he wakes up in the morning, he thinks 'Fuck! I shouldn't have done that!'

GORDON RAMSAY (1966–), www.saidwhat.co.uk

I'd sooner starve.

American actress JULIA ROBERTS (1967–), when asked if she would be tasting haggis during her visit to Scotland

'Lord, for what we are about to receive,
Help us to be truly thankful – Aimen –
Wumman, ye've put ingans in't again.'

TOM SCOTT (1918–85), *Auld Sanct Andrians*

The sauce-bottles are filled with old blood
above the off-white linen.

IAIN CRICHTON SMITH (1928–98), 'By the Sea'

'That fowl', says Brough to the landlady, 'is of a breed I know. I knew the cut of its jib whenever it was put down. That was the grandfather of the cock that frightened Peter.'
. . . 'Na-na, it's not so old,' says the landlady, 'but it eats hard.'

ROBERT LOUIS STEVENSON (1850–94), *Letters*, on a meal on Iona

A dense black substance, inimical to life.

ROBERT LOUIS STEVENSON, quoted in Iain Finlayson,
The Scots (1987), on 'black bun'

After an exotic meal (we recommend the legendary local roll and mince or alternatively, stovies and chips), why not sample some after dinner drinks in the local hostelries. It's easy to stagger round town afterwards and enjoy the local delights such as 'the Bingo' or why not catch a bus and travel to one of the many local retail parks to visit one of the 24hr Tesco's or Bingo Halls. Yes there's lots to do in this culturally diverse and vibrant city – did we mention the Bingo?

As you retire to your room in the early hours, listening to the fighting outside and the sound of police sirens, you can look forward to a delightful mouth-watering local continental breakfast the next morning – normally a roll and lorne served with chef's seasonal vegetables (potato scone) and tea.

From that first push at the intercom button at the entrance steps, followed by a resonant 'Whit Dya Want?' and 'Yer no takin yer Buckie in wi ye' to your first steps into the elaborate chipboard foyer with just a whiff of something you can't quite place, you will meet Big Betty the Maitre'De who will demand immediate payment in advance for your room. You can be rest-assured, the Great Eastern will cater for your every need and whim. Located nearby you will find a highly recommended chippy, off-sales and Curry House and lots of traditional rustic pubs and bars – all within a few minutes walk. Street security cameras will follow you on every step of your journey to ensure your safety. Now is the time to get your reservations made in advance of the rush. We guarantee you won't find anything else quite like it!

www.vomitscotland.com; A Glasgow hotel,
as described on VomitScotland website 2007.
'Lorne' is Lorne Sausage, a square-shaped charcuterie
item unique to Scotland. 'Buckie' is Buckfast Tonic Wine.

There is great store of fowl too, as foul houses, foul sheets, foul dishes and pots, foul trenchers and napkins . . . They have good store of fish too, and good for those that can eat it raw; but if it once come into their hands, it is worse than if it were three days old: for their butter and cheese, I will not meddle withal at this time, nor no man else at any time that loves his life.

SIR ANTHONY WELDON,
A Perfect Description of the People and Country of Scotland (1617)

In the old days, expat Scots used to inflict their cooking on the locals only once a year, on Burns Night. Then the Food and Drug Administration intercepted a Beverly Hills-bound consignment of haggis. Alarmed at the lab test results, officials reclassified the beloved dish as fertiliser.

It is now on a list of forbidden imports, along with nerve gas and nuclear weapons.

TIM WORSTALL, timworstall blog, 30 Aug 2005

Insulting terms: a select glossary

bampot: idiot
bass, bassa: bastard
bauchle: worthless, shambling person
bawheid: bald-headed person
bladdered: drunk
blate: shy, wimp-like
blether: chatterbox

gether-up: small, ill-dressed woman
glaikit: useless, feeble
gomeril: fool
gowk: fool (cuckoo)
hairy: another word for *senga* in some parts of Glasgow
haivers: nonsense, rubbish
hing-oot: dishevelled type

blether

hing·oot

carnaptious: argumentative
clag-tail: unwiped arse
clype: tell-tale
cuddie: donkey
dobber: idiot
dreep: feeble person
dreich: dull, grey, tedious
dreik: excrement
feartie: coward

Irish steak: cheese
jessie: effeminate man or boy; now obsolescent (Jessie was once one of the most popular names for a girl)

85

keelie: a city rough, especially from Glasgow

minger: a smelly person

ned: adolescent male in sports-type clothing who hangs about in public with similar types

nid: inhabitant of Niddrie district, Edinburgh

numpty: an idiot

numpty

nyaff: a useless, no-account fellow; usually 'wee' goes in front

nyuck: see *nyaff*

oof-lookin: stupid-looking

plookie: pimple-faced

radge: originally a tinkers' term for a non-tinker; now used as a general word of disparagement.

scadgie: someone who overdoes the temperament

scaffbag: rubbish bag

schemie: resident of a council housing estate

scunner: nuisance, annoyance, pest

senga: reverse form of Agnes – a female ned

shaan: no-good, hostile; a tinkers' term originally; often used with gadgie (fellow)

shaan gadgie: someone to be distrusted

shauchle-bodied: shaky

shilpit: feeble, shaky, sickly

snash: abusive language

stank dodger: skinny person (a stank is a drain grating)

sumph: great fool

teuchter: Urban and Lowland mock-Gaelic word for a Highlander; a hayseed, a bumpkin from the mountains

tumshie: idiot (literally, turnip)

Weegie: Glaswegian

wersh: insipid, tasteless; or the opposite: sharp, vinegary

The Kirk, God and the Devil

There is more knavery among kirkmen than honesty among courtiers.

Anonymous

An old tale from the west relates that St Columba and St Moluag were engaged in a race to be first to reach the isle of Lismore and convert its inhabitants to Christianity. Seeing Columba gaining, Moluag chopped off his little finger and threw it to land, thus claiming possession. Irked, Columba cried:

'May you have the alder for your firewood.'

'The Lord will make the alder burn pleasantly,' replied Moluag.

'May you have the jagged ridges for your pathway,' said Columba.

'The Lord will smooth them to the feet,' replied Moluag.

St Andreus is an Atheist, and Glasgow is ane gouke:
A wencher Brechin: Edinburgh of avarice a pocke:
To popery prone is Galloway: Dunkeld is rich in thesaure . . .
O quhat a shame Christ's flock to trust to such unfaithful dogs

Anonymous pasquil on the Scottish Bishops, from the 1630s

They'll know at Resurrection Day
To murder Saints was no sweet play.

From a C17th tomb in Glasgow Cathedral

An elderly Highlander, who had grown tired of the internecine squabbles and schisms of the small Presbyterian sect to which he had long belonged, confided to a friend: 'Sometimes I think I'll just give up religion altogether; and start going to the Church of Scotland.'

Traditional

A parish minister was reproving one of his parishioners for his frequent failures to come to the church service. The man muttered something about the services being 'too long', which annoyed the minister even more.

'One day, you know, you'll end up in a place where there are no sermons, either long or short,' he said.

'Aye, and maybe it won't be for a lack of ministers,' said the other.

Traditional

Thou knowest that the silly snivelling body is not worthy even to keep a door in thy house. Cut him down as a cumberer of the ground; tear him up root and branch, and cast the wild rotten stump out of the vineyard. Thresh him, o Lord, and dinna spare! O thresh him tightly with the flail of thy wrath, and mak a strae wisp of him to stap the mouth o' Hell.

Anonymous Seceder minister, preaching on the green at Symington, against the parish minister, quoted in Agnes Mure Mackenzie, *Scottish Pageant 1707–1802* (1950)

Pisky, Pisky, Amen,
Down on your knees and up again.

Rude boys' chant to Episcopalians, quoted in H. Grey Graham, *The Social Life of Scotland in the Eighteenth Century* (1899)

We thank thee, O Lord, for all thy mercies; such as they are.

> Anonymous Aberdeen minister,
> quoted in William Power, *Scotland and the Scots* (1934)

One is tempted almost to say that there was more of Jesus in St Theresa's little finger than in John Knox's whole body.

> MATTHEW ARNOLD (1822–88),
> *Literature and Dogma*

My father had a strong dislike for marriages of necessity, common enough at one time in Scotland. He was called to officiate at one of these, and arrived with reluctance and disgust half an hour late.

'You are very late, Mr Baird,' said the bridegroom.

'Yes, about six months too late,' replied Mr Baird.

> JOHN LOGIE BAIRD (1888–1946),
> *Sermons, Soap and Television, on his father*

> Let us exorcise
> the old god of Scotland
> with his knotted brain and jellyfish eyes
> who has tormented his children
> from generation unto generation.

> TOM BUCHAN (1931–95), 'Exorcism'

When the Scotch Kirk was at the height of its power, we may search history in vain for any institution which can compete with it, except the Spanish Inquisition.

> HENRY THOMAS BUCKLE (1821–62),
> *History of Civilisation in England*

As cauld a wind as ever blew,
A caulder kirk, and in't but few;
As cauld a preacher's ever spak'
Ye'll a' be het ere I come back.

ROBERT BURNS (1759–96),
'On a Church Service at Lamington'

An' now, auld 'Cloots', I ken ye're thinkin,
A certain bardie's rantin, drinkin,
Some luckless hour will send him linkin'
To your black pit;
But, faith! he'll turn a corner jinkin,
An' cheat you yet.

ROBERT BURNS (1759–96),
'Address to the Deil'

There is one place in the Universe where God and the Devil
join hands. That place is Scotland.

H.J. CAMERON (1873–c. 1930)

Begg belonged to the old native stock, the surliest, crassest and
most fanatical in Scotland. He was typical of the breed, a man
of mean intellect and little culture . . . a truculent and
vindictive bully whose influence in the councils of the Church
was won and maintained by a system of terrorism and coarse
intrigue.

DONALD CARSWELL, Brother Scots (1927),
on the Rev. James Begg, minister
of Newington Free Church

Mr —, you must cut out one half of that sermon. It doesn't matter which half.

DR THOMAS CHALMERS (1780–1847), in William Knight,
Some Nineteenth-Century Scotsmen (1903),
to an Edinburgh divinity student

King James VI was complaining of the leanness of his hunting horse, when his fool, Archy Armstrong, said he could tell how to make the horse fatter in a very short time.

'How is that?' said the king.

'Make him a bishop,' replied Archy, 'and if he is not soon as fat as he can wallow, then ride me!'

ROBERT CHAMBERS, *Scottish Jests and Anecdotes* (1832)

. . . not a religion for gentlemen

KING CHARLES II (1630–85), in Gilbert Burnet (1643–1715),
History of His Own Times; Charles is persuading his minister,
Lauderdale, to give up Presbyterianism for Episcopacy

Then the folk were sair pitten aboot,
An' they cried, as the weather grew waur:

'Oh Lord! We ken we hae sinn'd,
But a joke can be carried owre far!'
Then they chapped at the ark's muckle door,
To speir gin douce Noah had room;
But Noah never heedit their cries;
He said, 'This'll learn ye to soom.'

W.D. COCKER (1882–1970), 'The Deluge'

The minister (and Moderator of the Kirk) David Williamson, who lived in the latter part of the seventeenth century and the early eighteenth, enjoyed a special notoriety by having married no less than seven wives in succession. His contemporaries speculated freely on the reasons for his sexual prowess, the most popular suggestion being that he possessed three testicles:

. . . he made numerous converts, and its odd
Not more by preaching than his ponderous codd,
Or stone, that had of weight and vigour more
Than the other two he carried straight before;
The cause he finger'd them oft was not his choice,
But force to keep them in an equal poise. . .
After three score he married the seventh wife.
And to his dying day could mount his pole,
And like any old rat penetrat each hole.

MR FINNIE, 'Elegy on the Death of Williamson',
from James Maidment, *Scottish Pasquils* (1868)

. . . a base impudent brazen-faced villain, a spiteful ignorant pedant, a gross idolator, a mere slanderer, an evil man, hardened against all shame . . . full of insolence and abuse, chicanery and nonsense, detestable, misty, erroneous, wicked, vile, pernicious, terrible and horrid doctrines, tending to corrupt the mind and stupify the conscience, with gross iniquity, audacious hostility, pitiful evasion, base, palpable and shocking deceit

> REV. ADAM GIB (fl. C17th), anti-Burgher leader, reviewing
> a work by the Rev. Archibald Hill, a Burgher minister,
> from a pamphlet printed in Perth (1782)

Religion – a Scot know religion? Half of them think of God as a Scot with brosy morals and a penchant for Burns. And the other half are over damned mean to allow the Almighty even existence.

LEWIS GRASSIC GIBBON (James Leslie Mitchell, 1901–35), *Cloud Howe*

Three generations of one family were ministers – two of them university professors of divinity. The general view was that talent had declined in each stage. Someone mentioned to the Rev. Dr Gillan, of Paisley, that he had heard the grandson preach.

'What kind of a sermon was it?' asked Gillan. 'If it had both manner and matter, it would be the grandfaither's; if it had matter, but no manner, it would be the faither's; and if it had neither matter nor manner, it would be his ain.'

> From JOHN GILLESPIE, *Humours of Scottish Life*, 1904

Two rude boys in Dumfries shouted to to the minister, the Rev. Walter Dunlop, 'Hey, maister! The de'ils deid!'

To which he replied, 'In that case I must pray for two fatherless bairns.'

Recorded in Alexander Hislop, *The Book of Scottish Anecdote* (1883)

'I hope you are pleased with my preaching this afternoon, John,' said a vain young probationer to the beadle who was disrobing him in the vestry after the sermon.

'It was all sound, sir,' said John, with a sly expression.

Recorded in Alexander Hislop, *The Book of Scottish Anecdote* (1883)

... upon the whole, we may conclude, that the Christian Religion not only was at first attended by miracles, but even at this day cannot be believed by any reasonable person without one.

DAVID HUME (1711–76), *An Essay Concerning Human Understanding*

In all ages of the world, priests have been enemies of liberty.

DAVID HUME (1711–76), *Of the Parties of Great Britain*

What is betwixt the pride of a glorious Nebuch-adnezzar and the preposterous humility of our puritan ministers, claiming to their parity, and crying, 'We are all but vile worms'; and yet will judge and give law to their king, but will be judged nor controlled by none. Surely there is more pride under such a one's black bonnet than under great Alexander's diadem.

KING JAMES VI (1566–1625), *Basilikon Doron*

The High Church ... high only in the sense that game is high – when it is decomposing.

Attributed to LORD KELVIN (1824–1907), in Angela Cran and James Robertson, *Dictionary of Scottish Quotations* (1996)

I think Calvinism has done more harm to Scotland than drugs
ever did.

R.D. LAING (1927–89), speaking in Iona Abbey, 1984

. . . the minister's voice
spread a pollution of bad beliefs

NORMAN MACCAIG (1910–96), *Highland Funeral*

The Rev. Donald Maclean, minister of Oa in Argyll in the
early 20th century, was notoriously indolent in his duties. One
of his parishioners, Lachlan McNeil Weir, returned from an
appendix operation in Glasgow, went to the church for the
Sunday service and found it deserted. He went inside and rang
the bell. Presently the minister appeared, furious and indignant. Seeing Weir, he shouted:

'They took the guts oot o' ye in Glesga, but they didna take
the cheek!'

From COLIN MACDONALD, *Highland Journey* (1943)

Religion? Huh!

HUGH MACDIARMID (C.M. Grieve, 1892–1978), 'Two Memories'

I saw twa items on
The TV programme yesterday.
'General Assembly of the Church of Scotland'
Said ane – the ither 'Nuts in May'.
I lookit at the picters syne
But which was which I couldna say.

HUGH MACDIARMID (C.M. Grieve, 1892–1978), 'Nuts in May'

. . . incompetently strummed guitars and cringe-making,
smiley, cheesy foil groups . . . cultural vandalism . . . The
church has simply aped the secular West's obsession with
'accessibility', 'inclusiveness', 'democracy' and 'anti-elitism'.

The effect of this on liturgy has been a triumph of bad taste and banality and an apparent vacating of the sacred spaces of any palpable sense of the presence of God.

JAMES MACMILLAN (1959–) on modern church music,
quoted in *Scotland on Sunday*, 3 October 2006

As far as I'm concerned, Scotland will be reborn when the last minister is strangled with the last copy of the *Sunday Post*.

TOM NAIRN (1932–), 'The Three Dreams of Scottish Nationalism',
in Karl Miller, *Memoirs of a Modern Scotland* (1970)

I cannot praise the Doctor's eyes,
I never saw his glance divine;
He always shuts them when he prays,
And when he preaches I shut mine.

GEORGE OUTRAM (1806–50), recorded in Alexander Hislop,
The Book of Scottish Anecdote (1883)

I've read the secret name o' Knox's God,
The gowd calf 'Getting On'.

TOM SCOTT (1918–), 'Fergus'

O ay! the Monks! the Monks! they did the mischief!
Theirs all the grossness, all the superstition,
Of a most gross and superstitious age.

> Sir Walter Scott (1771–1832), *The Monastery*

What has the Kirk given us? Ugly churches and services, identifying in the minds of the churchgoers ugliness with God, have stifled the Scottish arts almost out of existence . . . Until the Kirk as it has been is dead Scotland will continue to be the Home of Lost Causes.

> George Scott-Moncrieff (1910–74), in D.C. Thomson,
> *Scotland in Quest of Her Youth: A Scrutiny* (1932)

Coatbridge youth Sean O'Brien (16) died recently whilst doing a Y.O.P. course at a factory. Sean (a good British name) went to dry himself at a heater unaware that his boiler suit was soaked in paraffin . . . Sean's father Dennis said it was a pity this had happened as Sean was just warming to the job . . . Sean disproved the old theory that Shite does not burn.

> 'Scottish Loyalist View, 1983–84', quoted in Steve Bruce,
> *No Pope of Rome* (1985)

Covenanters. Hopeless cases committed to hopeless causes. Ten thousand martyrs, but no saints.

> W. Gordon Smith, *Mr Jock* (1987)

A feckless crew, no worth a preen,
As bad as Smith o' Aiberdeen.

> Robert Louis Stevenson (1850–94), on a backsliding
> congregation; the Rev. W. Robertson Smith
> was tried for heresy by the Free Church

. . . a supernatural religion, whose roots cling deep in the past, whose branches and scions extend over all regions of the earth, whose evil shadow chills and darkens our richest fields of culture and civilisation

JAMES THOMSON (1834–82),
in the *National Reformer*, on Christianity

The Bischop wald nocht wed ane wyfe,
The Abbot not persew ane,
Thinkand it was ane lustie lyfe,
Ilk day to haif a new ane.

The Brothers Wedderburn, 'The Paip, That Pagane Full of Pryde',
from *Gude and Godlie Ballatis* (c. 1640)

God – a bad idea, but a fixed idea, and which has had a very long-winded, mind benumbing history in Scotland.

KENNETH WHITE (1936–), *On Scottish Ground*

. . . a pathological nightmare

KENNETH WHITE (1936–), *On Scottish Ground*,
on the Book of Revelation

Lairds, lords and toffs

Do ye not know who lyes in this corner?
It's a Scots Ambassador extraordinar . . .
Ladies, I request you, keep from the Wall,
Or the Scots Ambassador will occupy you all.

Anonymous lines on the Earl of Rothes (1600–c. 1641)

Stair's neck, mynd, wife, sons, grandson and the rest,
Are wry, false, witch, pests, parricid, possest

From 'Satyre on the Familie of Stairs', on Sir James Dalrymple, Viscount Stair (1619–95), and his family, early C18th

Curs'd be the Stars which did ordain
Queen Bess a maiden-life should reign;
Married, she might have brought an heir
Nor had we known a Stuart here.
Curs'd be the tribe who at Whitehall
Slew one o' th' name, and slew not all.

Anonymous English pasquinade against the Stewarts, c. 1680

A brat of an unburried Bitch,
Gott by Belzebub on a witch.

Anonymous epitaph on the First Earl of Stair (1648–1707), quoted in J. Maidment, *Book of Scottish Pasquils* (1866)

Open your doors, you devils, and prepare
A room that's warm for honest Lady Stair.

Anonymous, 'Upon the Long Wished-for and Tymely Death of the
Right Honourable the Lady Stair'

Thou soncie auld carle, the world hes not thy lyke,
For ladies fa' in love with thee, tho' thou be ane auld tyke.

Anonymous comment on the elderly Viscount Tarbat's marriage in
1700 to the younger Countess of Wemyss

Then up wi' Geordie, kirn-milk Geordie,
Up wi' Geordie high in a tow.
At the last kick of a foreign foot,
We'se a' be ranting roaring fou.

Anonymous, 'Kirn-milk Geordie', Jacobite song against George I
written after the 1715 Rebellion

Napoleon was an emperor,
He ruled by land and sea;
He was king of France and Germany,
But he ne'er ruled Polmadie.

Anonymous, 'Johnnie Lad'

Andrew Fletcher of Saltoun was notoriously short-tempered.
Unable to stand his master's rages, his butler gave notice.
'I cannot bear your temper, sir,' he said.
'Come now,' said Fletcher. 'It's no sooner on than it's off
again.'
'Na, sir, it's no sooner off than it's on again.'

Traditional

MacDonald of Keppoch was out with his men one snowy winter day, tracking down a party from a neighbouring clan who had raided Keppoch's barnyard for food. As it grew dark, they resolved to camp for the night rather than return home. The chief, looking around, asked one of his men to roll up a big ball of snow, so that he might have something to rest his head on. The clansmen, hearing this, shook their heads and muttered to one another: 'How will we ever have the victory in it when our chief is grown so effeminate he needs a pillow at night.'

Traditional

O Lord, keep my body frae the doctors, my purse frae the lawyers, my soul frae the deevil, and my dochters frae the Laird o' the Glen.

'Macma's Prayer', said to be uttered by tenants at Macma, Annandale

> may the perfume of her garden
> that she tells us is so famous
> turn sour as burning flesh
> and may her pink and white skin
> be stripped from her bones
> and spat to herring gulls

ELIZABETH BURNS (1957–), 'The Laird's Wife Visits the Poorhouse'

> You see yon birkie ca'd a lord,
> Wha struts, and stares, and a' that?
> Though hundreds worship at his word,
> He's but a coof for a' that.

ROBERT BURNS (1759–96), 'A Man's a Man For a' That'

What dost thou in that mansion fair?
Flit, Galloway, and find
Some narrow, dirty, dungeon cave,
The picture of thy mind . . .
Bright ran thy line, O Galloway,
Thro' many a far-fam'd sire;
So ran the far-fam'd Roman way,
And ended in a mire!

ROBERT BURNS (1759–96),
'Epigrams Against the Earl of Galloway'

But gentlemen, an' ladies warst,
Wi' ev'n-down want o' wark are curst.
They loiter, lounging, lank an' lazy;
Tho' deil-haet ails them, yet uneasy . . .
Ae night they're mad wi' drink an whuring,
Niest day their life is past enduring.

ROBERT BURNS (1759–96), *The Twa Dogs*

The injured Stuart line is gone,
A race outlandish fills their throne;
An idiot race, to honour lost;
Who know them best despise them most.

ROBERT BURNS (1759–96), 'Written By Somebody on the Window
of an Inn at Stirling. Looking up at the then semi-ruinous castle,
he inscribed these lines on the House of Hanover'

Strip your Louis XIV of his king gear and there is left nothing
but a poor forked radish with a head fantastically carved.

THOMAS CARLYLE (1795–1881), *On Heroes and Heroism*

. . . that proud chieftain of the pudding race, the Right
Honourable the Earl of Rosebery

> T.W.H. CROSLAND, *The Unspeakable Scot* (1902)

There you go for a damned cowardly Italian!

> Said to have been shouted by Lord Elcho on seeing
> Prince Charles Edward leave the field of Culloden, April 1746

From Hell he came in his beginning: his origin makes it easier
to believe the news, now that his existence is again prosperous
among the hot ash showers of the Devil.

> FIONNLAGH RUADH, Red Finlay (fl. C16th), from the Gaelic,
> on the death of Allan, Chief of Clanranald

Mention not the manly vigour of the man who went in to his
mother and to his sister.

> FIONNLAGH RUADH, Red Finlay (fl. C16th), from the Gaelic,
> on the death of Allan, Chief of Clanranald

The Duke then said he would like to hear the Gaelic talked in its
purity by two natives of the Highlands. He had a Highland piper
attached to his establishment whom he would call up if the
Doctor would kindly enter into conversation with him. Dr
McLeod said he would be delighted to do so; so the piper was
summoned and duly appeared. 'This is Dr McLeod,' said the
Duke. 'Ah, yes! your Grace, a' the Hielands ken Dr McLeod.'
Taking the initiative, and addressing the piper in Gaelic, the
Doctor said, 'Donald, he seems a decent sort of man this master
of yours?' Replying in the same language Donald rejoined, 'Hoot
aye, man, Doctor! but he's a great fool for a' that!'

> Told of Dr Norman McLeod and the Duke of Sussex,
> in John Gillespie, *The Humours of Scottish Life* (1904)

Derby is a very weak-minded fellow I am afraid, and, like the feather pillow, bears the marks of the last person who has sat on him. I hear he is called in London 'genial Judas'!

EARL HAIG (1861–1928), letter to his wife, on the Earl of Derby

Born into the ranks of the working class, the new King's most likely fate would have been that of a street-corner loafer.

JAMES KEIR HARDIE (1856–1915), on King George V, 1910

Generation after generation, these few families of tax-gatherers have sucked the life-blood of our nation; in their prides and lusts they have sent us to war, family against family, class against class, race against race; that they might live in idleness and luxury, the labouring mass has sweated and starved; they have pruned the creeds of our Church and stolen its revenues; their mailed fists have crushed the newer thought, and their vanities the arts.

TOM JOHNSTON (1881–1965), *Our Scots Noble Families*

Show the people that our Old Nobility is not noble, that its lands are stolen lands – stolen either by force or fraud, show people that their title-deeds are rapine, murder, massacre, cheating, or court harlotry . . . shatter the Romance that keeps the nation numb and spellbound while privilege picks its pockets.

TOM JOHNSTON (1881–1965), *Our Scots Noble Families*

. . . maid Regent in the year of God 1554; and a croune putt upone hir head, als seimlye a sight (yf men had eis) as to putt a saddil upon the back of ane unrewly kow

JOHN KNOX (c. 1507–72), *History of the Reformation in Scotland,*
on Mary of Guise, Regent 1554–60

. . . greater abomination was never in the nature of any woman than it is in her

JOHN KNOX (c. 1507–72), *History of the Reformation in Scotland,*
on Mary, Queen of Scots

We call hir nott a hoore . . . but sche was brought up in the company of hooremongaris (yea, of such as no more regarded incest, than honest men regard the company of their lauchfull wyeffis) . . . what sche was and is, her self best knowis, and God (we doubt nott) will farther declair.

JOHN KNOX (c. 1507–72), *History of the Reformation in Scotland,*
on Mary, Queen of Scots

John Knox
sharing a joke
with friends

Our gentyl men are all degenerate;
Liberalitie and Lawtie, both, are loste;
And Cowardice with lords is laureate;
And knichtlie curage turnit in brag and boast.

SIR DAVID LINDSAY (c. 1490–1555), *Dreme of the Realme of Scotland*

Oh, that boar, king George,
Son of the German sow;
His love for us is well-known –
'Tis the raven's for the bone.

ALEXANDER MACDONALD (Alasdair MacMaighstir Maighstir,
c. 1695–1770), 'Ais-eiridh na Sean Chanain Albannaich',
('Revival of the Old Scottish Speech'), 1751)

The daughter of a base and brainless breed
Is given what countless better women sorely need . . .
Rope in the shameless hussy, let her be
Directed to factory work or domestic service.
Along with all the other drones and spivs.

HUGH MACDIARMID (C.M. Grieve, 1892–1978),
'Royal Wedding Gifts', on public gifts to Princess Elizabeth, 1947

Henry VIII approached as nearly to the ideal standard of perfect
wickedness as the infirmities of human nature will allow.

SIR JAMES MACKINTOSH (1765–1832), *History of England*

Although Dunvegan nearly burned down
There was no 'nearly' in the burning of the houses
That MacLeod burned to keep Dunvegan
In grandeur on its rocks.

SORLEY MACLEAN (1911–96), 'Satire 1: The Castle on Fire',
from the Gaelic

Let Mitchell glorify God in the Grassmarket.

> JOHN MAITLAND, Duke of Lauderdale (1616–82), of
> James Mitchell, tried in 1678 for the attempted assassination
> of Archbishop Sharp, which he had done 'for the glory of God';
> the Grassmarket was the place of public execution in Edinburgh

Here lies the worst of kings and the most wretched of men in the whole kingdom.

> KING ROBERT III (c. 1340–1406), self-pronounced epitaph,
> from Walter Bower, *Scotichronicon*, from the Latin;
> King Robert asked to be buried in a dungheap

> Mak' your lick-fud bailie core
> Fa' down behint him – not afore,
> His great posteriors to adore,
> Sawney, now the king's come.

> ALEXANDER RODGER (1784–1846), 'Sawney, Now the King's Come',
> burlesque of Sir Walter Scott's 'Carle, Now the King's Come',
> on the occasion of King George IV's visit to Edinburgh in 1822

We know that the organised workers of the country are our friends. As for the rest, they don't matter a tinker's cuss.

> EMMANUEL SHINWELL (1884–1986), Speech to the
> Electrical Trades Union Conference, 1947

There goes a carriage with a 'B' outside and a wasp within.

> SYDNEY SMITH (1771–1845), on Lord Brougham's
> monogrammed carriage

The wisest fool in Christendom

> Attributed to DUC DE SULLY (1559–1641), on King James VI;
> also ascribed to King Henri IV of France

One need not dwell on the character of the reigning house, which, brought ignobly to the throne, has been consistently ignoble from the first until the accession of her present Most Gracious Majesty.

> JAMES THOMSON (1834–82), in *Cope's Tobacco Plant*, 1876

The Queen came by, she looked so sour you could have hung a jug on her mouth.

> CHRISTIAN WATT (1833–1923),
> the *Christian Watt Papers*,
> on Queen Victoria

The land and the people

Sanct Petir said to God in a sport word,
'Can ye nocht mak a Helandman of this hors turd?'
God turned owre the hors turd with his pykit staff
And up start a Helandman blak as on draff.
Quod God to the Helandman, 'Quhair wilt thou now?'
'I will doun in the Lawland, Lord, and thair steill a kow.'

Anonymous, 'How the First Hielandman of God
Was Made from Ane Hors Turd', (C16th)

Up wi' the souters o' Selkirk,
And down wi' the Earl o' Home.

Traditional, 'Up Wi' the Souters o' Selkirk'

Scotsmen ay reckon frae an ill hour.

Proverb

The tenancy is bad, but the devil is in the sub-tenancy.

Gaelic proverb

The men of Angus . . . have been growing potatoes so long that
the Golden Wonder has entered into their souls.

JOHN R. ALLAN, *Summer in Scotland* (1938)

Our worst enemies are our own kin in the east. They accepted
the domination of the Saxon. Got the superiority complex in so
doing, and no-one looks so disdainfully now on the west-
coaster as the east-coaster who has lost, or almost lost, his
Gaelic . . . a pure case of the fox that lost its tail.

> JOHN BANNERMAN (1870–1938), letter to his son, quoted in
> Bannerman, *The Memoirs of Lord Bannerman of Kildonan*

The two classes that mek ahl the mischief of the kintry are
weemen and meenisters.

> WILLIAM BLACK (1841–98), *Highland Cousins*

> I am a Doric stereotype –
> Abune ma brose I rift, [*belch*]
> I skirl an birl at echtsome reels,
> An darn ma hose fur thrift.

> SHEENA BLACKHALL, *Stagwyse* (1995)

The term Stot, as applied to the Scotchman, was, we believe,
first used in this magazine. . . In the first place a Stot is, most
frequently, a sour, surly, dogged animal. He retains a most
absurd resemblance to a Bull, and the absurdity is augmented
by the fact that he once absolutely was a Bull . . . Look him in
the face and you discern the malice of emasculation and the
cowardice of his curtailed estate.

> *Blackwood's Magazine*, September 1822

. . . land of the omnipotent No

> ALAN BOLD (1943–98), *A Memory of Death*

Scotland the wee, crêche of the soul,
of thee I sing,
land of the millionaire draper, whisky vomit
and the Hillman Imp.

TOM BUCHAN (1931–95), 'Scotland the Wee'

The summits of the highest are mostly destitute of earth; and
the huge naked rocks, being just above the heath, produce the
disagreeable appearance of a scabbed head . . . To cast one's
eye from an eminence toward a group of them, they appear
still one above the other, fainter and fainter, according to the
aerial perspective, and the whole of a dismal gloomy brown
drawing upon a dirty purple; and most disagreeable of all when
the heath is in bloom.

EDMUND BURT (c. 1695–1755), *Letters from a Gentleman in the
North of Scotland*, on the Scottish mountains

And well I know within that bastard land
Hath Wisdom's goddess never held command:
A barren soil where nature's germs, confin'd
To stern sterility can stint the mind,
Whose thistle well betrays the niggard earth,
Emblem of all to whom the land gives birth;
Each genial influence nurtured to resist,
A land of meanness, sophistry, and mist.

LORD BYRON (1788–1824), 'The Curse of Minerva'

As long as woods have sticks,
Cummings will play foul tricks

Cameron saw about the clan Cumming

And call they this Improvement? – to have changed,
My native Clyde, thy once romantic shore,
Where nature's face is banished and estranged,

And Heaven reflected in thy wave no more;
Whose banks, that sweetened May-day's breath before,
Lie sere and leafless now in summer's beam,
With sooty exhalations covered o'er;
And for the daisied green sward, down thy stream
Unsightly brick-lanes smoke, and clanking engines gleam.

THOMAS CAMPBELL (1777–1844), 'Lines on Revisiting a Scottish River'

A poor, barren country, full of continual broils, dissensions, massacrings: a people in the last stage of rudeness and destitution . . . It is a country as yet without a soul: nothing developed in it but what is rude, external, semi-animal.

THOMAS CARLYLE (1795–1881), *On Heroes*,
on pre-Reformation Scotland

During the greater part of their history, the Scottish nation were like the conies, a feeble folk who made their houses in the rocks.

DONALD CARSWELL, *Brother Scots* (1927)

Mandrag, mymmerkin, maid maister but in mows,
Thrys schield trumpir with one threid bair goun,
Say Deo mercy, or I cry the doun.

WILLIAM DUNBAR (c. 1460–c. 1520), 'The Flyting of Dunbar and
Kennedy', to Walter Kennedy

Land of polluted river,
Bloodshot eyes and sodden liver,
Land of my heart forever,
Scotland the Brave.

BILLY CONNOLLY (1942–), in Jonathan Margolis, *The Big Yin* (1994)

... pre-commercial Scotland, a land of brigands and bigots

NORMAN DOUGLAS (1868–1952), *Siren Land*

> The men o' the North are a' gone gyte,
> A' gone gyte thegither, o,
> The derricks rise to the Northern skies,
> And the past is gane forever, o.

SHEILA DOUGLAS,
'The Men of the North', in Gordon Wright,
Favourite Scots Lyrics (1973)

Well, it really is time to ... face up to some harsh realities.

1. Scotland is a small, sparsely populated appendage of England. Those who called it 'North Britain' in the 18th century had it right.
2. The weather is impossibly wet.
3. Most of the land north of Loch Lomond is barren rock.
4. Scotland lost its political independence 300 years ago and the creation of a Scottish Parliament, a glorified county council housed in a risible and over-priced folly of a building, has not restored it.
5. Educational standards in Scotland, once the highest in Europe, have – with a few exceptions – collapsed.
6. When it comes to sport – and I do not count the one decent tennis player – Scotland is the Belarus of the West.
7. In fact, when it comes to just about everything, it is the Belarus of the West.
8. That is why so many Scots emigrate. As I did.

NIALL FERGUSON, *The Daily Telegraph*,
31 December 2005

I think the Scots are a lazy set of bastards, to be quite frank . . . I
don't think the work ethic is very strong.

SIR MONTY FINNISTON (1912–91), quoted in Kenneth Roy,
Conversations in a Small Country (1989)

They are not, to put it as tactfully as possible, the most
immediately lovable folk in the United Kingdom.

GEORGE MACDONALD FRASER, *Steel Bonnets* (1971), on the Borderers

. . . the most interesting nicknames . . . were those descriptive
and often highly offensive appellations referring to personal
appearance, habits and behaviour. Thus we find Curst Eckie,
Ill Will Armstrong, Nebless Clem Croser, the two Elliott
brothers, Archie and George, who were familiarly known as
'Dog Pyntle' and 'Buggerback'.

GEORGE MACDONALD FRASER, *The Steel Bonnets* (1971)

. . . the Scots countryside itself, fathered between a kailyard
and a bonny brier bush in the lee of a house with green shutters

LEWIS GRASSIC GIBBON (James Leslie Mitchell, 1901–35), *Sunset Song*

Nobody knows what the original people of Scotland were
– cold is probably the best
informed guess, and wet.

A.A. GILL (1954–)

It is not uncommon to see men and women staggering home blind drunk at the end of a night out — singing, shouting or fighting as they go. This is accepted behaviour in Scotland. Drinking to excess is not only acceptable, it is virtually expected.

JAMIE GRANT, *The Cultureshock Guide to Scotland* (2006)

It is common for Scots to insult each other with lots of foul language. If someone calls you names don't take offence. It is more than likely they are just being friendly.

JAMIE GRANT, *The Cultureshock Guide to Scotland* (2006)

The truth is we are a nation of arselickers, though we disguise it with surfaces: a surface of generous, openhanded manliness, a surface of dour practical integrity, a surface of futile maudlin defiance like when we break goalposts and windows after football matches on foreign soil and commit suicide on Hogmanay by leaping from fountains in Trafalgar Square.

ALASDAIR GRAY (1934–), *1982 Janine*

. . . we should be cautious when we assume we are unique. Other people may be just as crazy as we are.

CLIFF HANLEY (1922–99), 'A State of Mind', in *Sunday Mail Story of Scotland* (1988)

Presumably because of nationalist successes at the polls, men I thought had slunk away to prickly sulks on couches of thistles or even to realise in which decade of which century they lived in, came breengin' hurriedly back, reknitting their half-un-ravelled claymores, and pulling behind them pramfuls of young poets waving tartan rattles.

ALAN JACKSON (1938–), 'The Knitted Claymore',
in *Lines Review* (June 1971)

As for the Highlands, I shortly comprehend them all in two sorts of people: the one, that dwelleth in our mainland, that are barbarous for the most part, and yet mixed with some show of civility: the other that dwelleth in the Isles, and are utterly barbarous.

KING JAMES VI (1566–1625),
Basilikon Doron

Our gentyl men are all degenerate;
Liberalitie and Lawtie, both are lost;
And cowardice with lordis is laureate;
And knichtlie courage turnit in brag and boast.

SIR DAVID LINDSAY (c. 1490–1555),
'The Complaint of the Commoun Weill of Scotland'

. . . swordless Scotland, sadder than its psalms,
Fosters its sober youth on national alms
To breed a dull provincial discipline,
Commerce its god, and golf its anodyne.

ERIC LINKLATER (1899–1974), in Hugh MacDiarmid,
Lucky Poet (1943)

. . . they contracted ideas and habits, quite incompatible with the customs of regular society and civilized life, adding greatly to those defects which characterize persons living in a loose and unreformed state of society

JAMES LOCH (1780–1855), architect of the Sutherland clearances, in Ian Grimble, *The Trial of Patrick Sellar* (1962), giving his views on the inhabitants of Sutherland

Scotland's Image? You must be joking!
The less said about that the better . . .
Scotland's image? The hell with it!
I love, I curse, I hate, I care
that we alone should dare submit
we are to what we think we were!

TYRELL MCCONALL (1941–),
quoted in M. Lindsay,
Scotland: An Anthology (1974)

Nearly all the prominent people in Scottish public life today . . . remind me of the oxpeckers, an African genus of starlings. These birds are parasitic on the large mammals whose bodies they search for ticks and other vermin . . . So strikingly prehensile are their claws that Millais relates that when 'a dead bird that had grown stiff was thrown on the back and sides of an ox, so that the feet touched the animal's hide, the claws held fast at once, and could not easily be withdrawn'. That is precisely the relationship of most of these people (all dead – born dead, in fact) to Scottish life.

HUGH MACDIARMID
(C.M. Grieve, 1892–1978), *Lucky Poet*

You remember the place called the Tawny Field?
It got a fine dose of manure;
Not the dung of sheep and goats
But Campbell blood, well congealed.

IAIN LOM MACDONALD (c. 1620–c. 1707), 'Las Inbhir Lochaidh'
(The Battle of Inverlochy), translated from the
Gaelic by Derick Thomson

All you folks are off your head
I'm getting rich from your sea bed.
I'll go home when I see fit
All I'll leave is a heap of shit.

JOHN MCGRATH (1935–2002), *The Cheviot, the Stag, and the Black, Black Oil*

The Scottish Celts . . . like all peoples preponderantly peasant
in outlook, they worship money and titles.

ALASDAIR ALPIN MACGREGOR, *The Western Isles* (1949)

. . . morals, in the sexual sense, are extremely lax in the
Western Isles . . . Bastardy has long been common – nay
notorious – in the Highlands and Islands.

ALASDAIR ALPIN MACGREGOR, *The Western Isles* (1949)

Soap and water . . . have never found much favour in these
parts . . . That anyone should want even one bath a week, they
consider extraordinary: that anyone should desire a bath on
two consecutive days, is, to them, indicative of some regret-
table abnormality, if not actually a sign of daftness.

ALASDAIR ALPIN MACGREGOR, *The Western Isles* (1949)

My blessing with the foxes dwell,
For that they hunt the sheep so well.
Ill fare the sheep, a grey-fac'd nation
That swept our hills with desolation.

DUNCAN BÀN MACINTYRE (1724–1812),
'Song to the Foxes', from the Gaelic

A jocular anecdote of old blind Mr Stewart (of Appin). The
boy who was reading to him from the Book of Job mispro-
nounced the word camels. – 'If he had so many Cawmells in
his household,' said Mr Stewart, 'I do not wonder at his
misthriving.'

HENRY MACKENZIE (1745–1831),
The Anecdotes and Egotisms of Henry Mackenzie,
a dig at Clan Campbell

Lowland Scots and Covenanters
Do the same as Stewart kings:
Give them a London title,
And their back's to Edinburgh.

DONALD MACINTYRE (1889–1964),
'When the Stone Was Returned',
from the Gaelic

No other country has fallen so hard for its own image in the
funfair mirror. Tartan rock, and a Scottie dog for every pot.

CANDIA MACWILLIAM (1957–), *A Case of Knives*

Of Liddisdale the common thievis
Sa pertlie stealis now and reivis,
That nane may keep
Horse, nolt, nor sheep,
Nor yet dar sleep for their mischiefis.

SIR RICHARD MAITLAND (1496–1586),
'Aganis the Thievis of Liddisdale'

Scottish streets are given an atmosphere of their own simply by
the number of drunk people that one encounters in them.

EDWIN MUIR (1887–1959), *Scottish Journey*

If Freud had known anything about Scotland he would have
left Vienna like an arrow and taken on the whole population as
a collective patient, to treat the national neurosis, the com-
pulsive obsessive rigidity that permeates the population.

ALASTAIR REID (1926–), *Whereabouts* (1987)

. . . their wizened little country

ALASTAIR REID, *Whereabouts* (1987)

. . . that plateau of uncomfortable, grunt-punctuated silence
which Borderers seem to inhabit most of the time

ALASTAIR REID (1926–), 'Borderlines', in K. Miller,
Memoirs of a Modern Scotland (1971)

There's nought in the Highlands but syboes and leeks,
And long-legged callants gaun wantin' the breeks.

SIR WALTER SCOTT (1771–1832),
David Gellatley's song, from *Waverley*

This is the land God gave to Andy Stewart.

IAIN CRICHTON SMITH (1928–98), 'The White Air of March'

Oh, that's Scotland. All the families are odd, very odd.

WILLIAM SOUTAR (1898–1943), *Symposium*

. . . a Stewart, nae doubt – they all hing together like bats in a steeple

ROBERT LOUIS STEVENSON (1850–1894), *Kidnapped*

Ah don't hate the English. They're just wankers. We're colonised by wankers . . . We're ruled by effete arseholes. What does that make us? The lowest of the fuckin low . . . the most wretched, servile, miserable pathetic trash that was ever shat intae creation. Ah don't hate the English. They just git oan wi the shite thuv goat. Ah hate the Scots.

IRVINE WELSH (1958–), *Trainspotting*

The languages

The accent of the lowest state of Glaswegians is the ugliest one can encounter . . . it is associated with the unwashed and the violent.

> Anonymous university lecturer, quoted in Janet Menzies,
> *Investigation of Attitudes to Scots and Glaswegian Dialect*
> *Among Secondary School Pupils* (1975)

That laddie has clean tint [*lost*] his Scotch, and found nae English.

> LORD BRAXFIELD (1722–99) of Francis Jeffrey,
> later to be editor of the *Edinburgh Review*,
> when he came back from Oxford University

Good God! I hope not. I would rather the country was sunk in the sea. I, the Scotch accent!

> LORD BYRON (1788–1824), in E.C. Mayne,
> *Byron* (1924), on being told he had a slight Scots accent

Great the blindness and the sinful darkness and ignorance and evil will of those who teach, write and foster the Gaelic speech; for to win for themselves the empty rewards of the world, they both choose and use more and more to make vain and misleading tales, lying and worldly, of the Tuath de

Dannan, of fighting men and champions, of Fionn Mac-Cumhal and his heroes, and many more whom now I will not number.

JOHN CARSWELL, Kirk Superintendent of Argyll (fl. mid C16th),
Introduction to a Gaelic translation of the Liturgy of the English
Congregation at Geneva, from the Gaelic

When Andrew Melville, later the leader of the Presbyterian reformers, became professor of Latin at the University of Geneva, 'his Scottish stubbornness, in defending his own pronunciation of Greek, roused the wrath of the professor of that language, who was a native of Greece. '*Vos Scotti, vos barbari!*' he indignantly exclaimed, '*docebitis nos Graecos pronunciationem linguae nostrae, scilicet?*' (You barbarian Scots, will you teach us Greeks the way to speak our own language, then?')

JOHN EDGAR, *History of Early Scottish Education* (1893)

If an announcer pronounces 'Boer War' with the accent of Barra or the accent of Buchan, fair enough, but if he pronounces 'Boer War' as if he were a Pekingese barking defiance (baw waw! baw waw!) he should be out on his neck.

HAMISH HENDERSON (1920–2002), letter to
The Scotsman, 9 February 1953

John Clerk was arguing a Scotch appeal case before the House of Lords. His client claimed the use of a millstream by prescriptive right. Mr Clerk spoke broad Scotch, and argued that 'the watter had run that way for forty years. Indeed, naebody kenned how long, and why should his client now be deprived of the watter,' etc. The Chancellor, much amused at the pronunciation of the Scottish advocate, asked him, in rather a bantering tone, 'Mr Clerk, do you spell water in

Scotland with two t's?' Clerk was a little nettled at this hit at his national accent, and answered, 'Na, my lord, we dinna spell water with twa t's; but we spell mainners wi' twa n's.'

ALEXANDER HISLOP, *The Book of Scottish Anecdote* (1883),
on John Clerk (1757–1832)

'Learn English!' he exclaimed, 'no, never, it was my trying to learn that language that spoiled my Scots.

DR JOHN LEYDEN (1775–1811), in John Reith, *The Life of Dr John Leyden*;
on his arrival at Bombay, Leyden had been asked to speak 'English'

Of course, everyone knows the Dundonian phrase, 'oh meh, whit a dreh peh', but listening in on two Dundonians in full rant is quite something to experience. Because I'm from Perth people say I sound posh but I certainly don't consider that to be true.

'LINDA FROM PERTH', www.bbc.co.uk/whereIlive, Jan 2007

How could he compose a song
lacking skill and native wit?
. . . in the splutter of talk he produces
There is no man living that understands his Gaelic.

DUNCAN BÀN MACINTYRE (1724–1812),
'Aoir Uisdean' ('Satire on Hugh')

Highland Boatman: How do you do, Mr Pimmal, mho chulain goalich. What you no understand that chulain goalich, you're fine whelp.

Joe Pimple: Fine whelp! de'il speed your manners.

Boatman: What, did I put anger on you? A loah mo chriodh, Mr Pimmel.

Joe Pimple: What do you say? Speak English.

Boatman: I say loah mo chriodh, that's you're good calf.

Mrs Pimple: Good calf: gae oot o' this house, Sir.

Boatman: Oh gie's a pardon, Mrs Pimpall, I love speak Earse, that I no forget. No bheoch boch'd.

Mrs Pimple: Beo bo, What's that?

Boatman: Beoch, boch'd, that you're a poor beast, Mr Pimpall . . . are you making a laugh upon my languash? damme if I sink you give me any of your shaw, I make my stick dance a shig upon your skull.

ARCHIBALD McLAREN, *The Humours of Greenock Fair* (c. 1788)

You could drive a train across the Firth of Forth on her vowels.

BRUCE MARSHALL (1899–1987), *Teacup Terrace*

. . . none can more sincerely wish a total extinction of the Scottish colloquial dialect than I do, for there are few modern Scoticisms which are not barbarisms.

JOHN PINKERTON (1758–1826), Preface to *Ancient Scottish Poems* (1786)

'Use my speech,' said the muse of Scotia:
. . . 'tis gude auld Scots I mean,
Your soudland gnaps I count not worth a preen.'
[*southern mincing talk, pin*]

ALEXANDER ROSS (1699–1784), *Helenore*

Many people think that Scots possesses a rich vocabulary, but this is a view not wholly borne out by a close examination . . . It is as if the Doric had been invented by a cabal of scandal-mongering beldams, aided by a council of observant game-keeepers.

GEORGE MALCOLM THOMSON, *The Re-Discovery of Scotland* (1928)

The Fort William accent is a kind of weird halfway between Glasgow and Inverness. It's not as nasal (or unpleasant) as Invernessian but not as fast or aggressive as Glaswegian.

MIKE WATTS, www.bbc.co.uk/whereIlive, of Fort William

Law and lawmen

If the Lord Chancellor knew only a little law, he would know a little of everything.

> Anonymous comment on Lord Brougham (1778–1868),
> in G.W.E. Russell, *Collections and Recollections* (1898)

Lord Brougham

A great deal rests on this gentleman's credibility. He is a Jew and may be an atheist. We are honest Scots. What faith can we put in this 'gentleman's' words?

> Advocate for the defence in the trial for murder of the trades
> unionist Alfred French, quoted in Peter Slowe, *Manny Shinwell* (1993),
> referring to Emmanuel Shinwell, a key witness, and later a senior
> Labour politician

Ye're a verra clever chiel, man, but ye wad be nane the waur o' a hanging.

> Alleged remark by LORD BRAXFIELD (1722–99), to a defendant,
> quoted in J.G. Lockhart, *Memoirs of the Life of Sir Walter Scott* (1837–38)

Muckle he made o' that – he was hanget.

> LORD BRAXFIELD (1722–99), quoted by Lord Cockburn
> in *Memorials of His Time* (1856), a sotto-voce comment,
> during a political trial, on the remark that
> Jesus Christ also was a reformer

Lord Braxfield

> A fig for those by law protected!
> Liberty's a glorious feast!
> Courts for cowards were erected,
> Churches built to please the priest.

> ROBERT BURNS (1759–96), 'The Jolly Beggars'

When Lord Meadowbank was yet Mr Maconochie, he one day approached his facetious professional brother, John Clerk of Eldin, and after telling him he had prospects of being raised to the bench, asked him to suggest what title he should adopt. 'Lord Preserve Us,' said Clerk, and moved off.

> ROBERT FORD, *Thistledown* (1901)

On a change of ministry, Henry Erskine was appointed to follow Henry Dundas as Lord Advocate. On the morning of his appointment, he met Dundas in the Parliament House . . . Erskine remarked that he must be off to order his silk gown.

' 'Tis not worth your while,' said Dundas, 'for the short time you'll want it, you had better borrow mine.'

'I have no doubt your gown,' replied Erskine, 'is made to fit any party; but however short may be my time in office, it shall not be said that Henry Erskine put on the abandoned habits of his predecessor.'

ROBERT FORD, *Thistledown* (1901)

God help the people who have such judges.

CHARLES JAMES FOX (1749–1806), on the Scottish Court of Session, at the time of the political trials of the 1790s

Fare ye a' weel, ye bitches.

LORD KAMES (1696–1782), to his fellow-judges, on leaving the Court of Session; 'bitch' appears to have been applicable to either sex

On the Ayrshire circuit, [Lord Kames] had occasion to sentence to death, for murder, one Matthew Hay. Kames and Hay had played chess together on some previous social occasion. Now, as the judge collected up his papers, he is reputed to have bent his head to Hay's advocate and murmured: 'There's checkmate to you, Matthew.'

A judge has sentenced himself to a suicide's grave?
– The nearest to a just sentence any judge ever gave.

HUGH MACDIARMID (C.M. Grieve, 1892–1978),
'A Judge Commits Suicide'

An advocate complaining to his friend, an eminent legal functionary of the last century, that his claims to a judgeship had been overlooked, added acrimoniously, 'and I can tell you they might have got a waur,' to which the only answer was a grave 'Whaur?'

> DEAN E.B. RAMSAY (1793–1872),
> *Reminiscences of Scottish Life and Character*

. . . that bastard verdict, 'Not Proven'. I hate that Caledonian *medium quid*. One who is not proven guilty is innocent in the eye of the law.

> SIR WALTER SCOTT (1771–1832), *Journal*

> Here enter not Attorneys, Barristers,
> Nor bridle-champing Law-practitioners:
> Clerks, Commissaries, Scribes nor Pharisees,
> Wilful disturbers of the people's ease . . .
> Your salary is at the gibbet-foot:
> Go drink there.

> SIR THOMAS URQUHART (1611–60), translation from Rabelais,
> *Gargantua and Pantagruel*

Men

Can spirit from the tomb, or fiend from Hell
More hateful, more malignant be, than Man?

JOANNA BAILLIE (1762–1851), 'Orra'

Every man who is high up loves to think he has done it himself:
and the wife smiles, and lets it go at that.

SIR J.M. BARRIE (1860–1937), *What Every Woman Knows*

The Scottish hardman, a human being trying to be a walking
prick, has had his day and dreadful it has been.

ALAN BOLD (1943–98), *The Sensual Scot*

Thomas Carlyle

What is man? a foolish baby;
Vainly strives, and fights, and frets;
Demanding all, deserving nothing,
One small grave is all he gets.

THOMAS CARLYLE (1795–1881), 'Cui Bono'

But anyhow it wasn't a woman who betrayed Jesus with a kiss.

CATHERINE CARSWELL (1879–1946), *The Savage Pilgrimage*

Men, even the good ones, are kittle cattle; God didn't give them much sense, and it's the woman's job to make the best of them.

O. DOUGLAS (Anna Buchan, 1877–1948), *Jane's Parlour*

The curse of Scotland is these wee hard men. I used to blame the English for our mediocrity. I thought they had colonised us by sheer cunning. They aren't very cunning. They've got more confidence and money than we have, so they can afford to lean back and smile while our own wee hard men hammer Scotland down to the same dull level as themselves.

ALASDAIR GRAY, *1982 Janine* (1984)

Says she, 'Guid men I've kistit twa,
But a change o' deils is lichtsome, lass.'

VIOLET JACOB (1863–1946), 'A Change o' Deils'

. . . men were just a perfect nuisance, wasn't that so, now?

JESSIE KESSON (1915–94), *A Glitter of Mica*

Two characteristics of the people, which the stranger to the Western Isles is swift to observe, certainly so far as the male population is concerned, are laziness and drunkenness.

ALASDAIR ALPIN MACGREGOR, *The Western Isles* (1949)

Mr —, in the Kyle, Ca'd me a common —:
But if he hadna tried himsel',
He wadna be so sure.

ISOBEL PAGAN (1741–1821), 'Lines on Mr —'

The Scarlet Whore, indeed, they snarl at,
But like right well a whore in scarlet

ALLAN RAMSAY (1686–1758),
'Epistle to Mr H.S. at London'

My mother asked a somewhat rhetorical question: how do you keep men happy? 'You have to feed 'em at both ends,' replied my grandmother.

MURIEL SPARK (1918–2006), *Curriculum Vitae*

One-off demolition jobs

On Africa

I take it Africa was brought about in sheer ill humour. No one can think it possible that an all-wise God (had he been in his sober senses) would create a land and fill it full of people destined to be replaced by other people from across the seas.

R.B. CUNNINGHAME GRAHAM (1852–1936), 'Bloody Niggers', from *Selected Writings*, edited by Cedric Watt (1981)

On the Albert Monument, London

. . . a monument whereat the nations stand aghast

NORMAN DOUGLAS (1868–1952)

On Americans

Aye, they have a great population, viz. 21 millions of the greatest bores that the moon ever saw.

DAVID LIVINGSTONE (1813–73), letter to his parents, 26 September 1852

On the animal kingdom

> Whae's like us? –
> Damned few,
> an'
> we're
> aw
> deid.

DOUGLAS LIPTON (1953–), 'Great Auk'

On Archbishop Laud

'Great praise to God, and little Laud to the Devil'.

ARCHIE ARMSTRONG (fl. C17th), court jester to King Charles I

On Argyll men

Argyleshire stots make the stupidest jurymen.

LORD COCKBURN (1779–1854), *Circuit Journeys*

On a BBC Announcer

At least he shall never read the Epilogue.

LORD REITH (1889–1971), head of the BBC,
when persuaded not to sack an announcer
who had been divorced, quoted in Ned
Sherrin, *Theatrical Anecdotes* (1991)

On booksellers

. . . if you would knock any brains into a bookseller you would
have my consent, but not to knock out any part of the portion
with which Heaven has endowed them

SIR WALTER SCOTT (1771–1832), letter to James Hogg, 1820

On boys

All my life I have loved a womanly woman and admired a manly man, but I never could stand a boily boy.

LORD ROSEBERY (1847–1929)

On the British honours system

It must be about the best honours system that money can buy.

JIMMY REID (1932–)

On the Burns cult

We went to the Cottage, and took some whisky . . . Oh, the flummery of a birth-place. Cant! cant! cant! It is enough to give a spirit the guts-ache.

JOHN KEATS (1795–1821), *Letters*, on a visit to Burns's birthplace

On businessmen

People of the same trade seldom meet together even for merriment and diversion but the conversation ends in a conspiracy against the public, or in some contrivance to raise prices.

ADAM SMITH (1723–90), *The Wealth of Nations*

On a Caithnessian

He seems a fine enough loon but ye can never tell with a Gallagh. Ye canna understand what they say half the time.

GEORGE GUNN, *The Gold of Kildonan* (1989)

On the common people

Who o'er the herd would wish to reign,
Fantastic, fickle, fierce, and vain?
. . . Thou many-headed monster-thing,
O who would wish to be thy king?

Sir Walter Scott (1771–1832),
The Lady of the Lake

On consensus and conformity

Scotland needs more consensus and conformity like it needs a hole in the head.

James MacMillan (1959–)

On conscription

Fat civilians wishing they
'Could go and fight the Hun.'
Can't you see them thanking God
That they're over forty-one?

E.A. MacKintosh (1893–1917),
'Recruiting'

On critics

Every critic in the town
Runs the minor poet down;
Every critic – don't you know it?
Is himself a minor poet.

R.F. Murray (1863–94)

On Darwinism

I have no patience whatever with these gorilla damnifications of humanity.

THOMAS CARLYLE (1795–1881), on Charles Darwin's
The Origin of Species

On experience

Experience teaches
That it doesn't.

NORMAN McCAIG (1910–96), 'Bruce and that Spider – the Truth'

On the folk tradition

. . . the boring doggerel of analphabetic and ineducable farm-labourers, tinkers and the like

HUGH MacDIARMID (C.M. Grieve, 1892–1978),
letter to *The Scotsman*, 9 January 1960

On fortune

Ne'er mind how Fortune waft and warp;
She's but a bitch.

ROBERT BURNS (1759–96), 'Second Epistle to J. Lapraik'

On the future

The future is not what it used
to be.

SIR MALCOLM RIFKIND,
in *Talking Politics*, BBC Radio,
1988

On gay men

We don't get God saying, 'Poor little gay men, we'll have to open the church hall and let them have their own little gay church and their own gay minister.'

God says, 'To death with them.'

Pastor Jack Glass, quoted in Steve Bruce, *No Pope of Rome* (1985)

On Glasgow's new water supply

I just canna thole that new water: it's got neither taste nor smell.

Old Glaswegian lady, quoted in Elizabeth Haldane,
The Scotland of Our Fathers (1933)

On grouse shooters

The grouse shooters were often rather pathetic people, going through a ritual imposed on them because they could afford it . . . They were stung, by everything and by everybody.

John R. Allan, *Farmer's Boy* (1935)

On halitosis

His breath's like a burst lavy, ye could strip paint wi' it.

Tony Roper, *The Steamie* (1987)

On handwriting

The dawn of legibility in his handwriting has revealed his utter inability to spell.

Attributed to Ian Hay (John Hay Beith, 1876–1952),
of a school report

On the Hebrideans

... many an Islander is seldom fully awake much before noon! If the pubs be open then or shortly afterwards, it is doubtful whether, on certain days, he is ever entirely in full possession of his faculties. Drink certainly exaggerates his temperamental laziness.

ALASDAIR ALPIN MACGREGOR,
The Western Isles (1949)

On heroism

In all the human societies we have ever reviewed, in every age and in every state, there has seldom if ever been a shortage of eager young males prepared to kill and die to preserve the security, comfort and prejudices of their elders, and what you call heroism is just an expression of this fact; there is never a scarcity of idiots.

IAIN BANKS (1954–), *Use of Weapons*

On Highlanders

'Now,' Bonnie Prince Charlie is reputed to have said, on first donning the kilt, 'now I should be a complete Highlander, if only I had the itch.'

G.S. FRASER (1915–80), *Scotland*

On history

History's easy. Dead easy. Very dead and very easy.

W. GORDON SMITH, *Mr Jock* (1987)

On humanitarians

They are all alike, these humanitarian lovers of first causes. Always ready to burn something, or somebody; always ready with their cheerful Hell-fire and gnashing of teeth.

> NORMAN DOUGLAS (1868–1952), *Old Calabria*

On incest (and folk-dancing)

You should make a point of trying every experience once, except incest and folk-dancing.

> 'Anonymous Scotsman' quoted by Sir Arnold Bax
> in *Farewell My Youth* (1943)

On industrial improvement

> We cam na here to view your warks,
> In hopes to be mair wise,
> But only, lest we gang to hell,
> It may be no surprise.

> ROBERT BURNS (1759–96), 'Impromptu on Carron Ironworks'

On inventing

Of all things in life there is nothing more foolish than inventing.

> JAMES WATT (1736–1819), quoted in
> H.W. Dickinson, *James Watt* (1936)

On Julius Caesar

> Great Julius, that trubute gat of a'
> His winning was in Scotland bot fu' sma'

> 'BLIND HARRY' (fl. 1490s) *The Wallace*

On life

> First braith
> Beginning o' yer daith.

Scots proverbial saying

On the Lumpen Scot

Make way for the Lumpen Scot. Habitat: largely the West of Scotland but found in large numbers across the country. Predominantly, but not exclusively male, traits are: aggressive, pig ignorant, loud, sexist. Health: one in two will contract cancer of some form, and his testicles are a carcinogenic war zone. Lifestyle: inert. Culture: football, football and football. Prospects: redundancy. Age: immaterial. Fears: profound sense of sexual and social insecurity – hates gays and English.

Sunday Herald, 23 April 2000

On metaphysics

The science appeared to me an elaborate, diabolical invention for mystifying what was clear, and confounding what was intelligible.

W.E. AYTOUN (1813–65)

On millionaires

A millionaire's just a shameless thief.

MARY BROOKSBANK (1897–1980),
'To the Erudite'

On Mons Meg

... a monument of our pride and poverty. The size is immense, but six smaller guns would have been made at the same expense, and done six times as much execution as she could have done.

SIR WALTER SCOTT (1771–1832), *Journal*

On museums

The blood runs cold at the very mention of a new museum in Scotland. Museums are Scotland's cancer; Edinburgh has terminal museum-tumours. There are museums for absolutely everything – whisky, tartan, sharp metal things, ghosts, the police, weaving, murder. There are probably museums devoted to spitting, facial hair, cobblestones, belly-button fluff and giving directions in a very slow voice. Scotland doesn't have a history; it has tea towels.

A.A. GILL (1954–)

On the name Grizel

... for some strange reason I can never hear it pronounced without thinking of a Polar bear eating an Eskimo

LEWIS GRASSIC GIBBON (James Leslie Mitchell, 1901–35), *Scottish Scene*

On nations

Most nations are forgeries, perpetrated in the last century or so.

NEAL ASCHERSON (1932–), *The Observer*, 1985

On a neds' website

. . . the usual melange of bad spelling, acne, Buckfast and a vague atmosphere of threat

STEWART KIRKPATRICK, *The Scotsman*, 17 December 2003

On Niagara Falls

Naething but a perfect waste o' watter.

Anonymous citizen of Paisley

On an officer

. . . at school that symbol o' extermination was called Fozie Tam

JAMES HOGG (1770–1835), in Christopher North,
'Noctes Ambrosianae', *Blackwood's Magazine*, 1835

On oil-men

Hammered like a bolt
diagonally through Scotland (my
small dark country) this
train's a
swaying caveful of half–
seas over oilmen (fuck
this fuck that fuck
everything) bound for Aberdeen and
North Sea Crude

LIZ LOCHHEAD (1947–), 'Inter-City'

On orangeism

. . . one of the least edifying brands of virulent religious fanaticism. Orangeism is alien to the Scottish tradition. Its mythology is a farrago of unhistorical balderdash.

HAMISH HENDERSON (1920–2002), letter to the
Edinburgh Evening Dispatch, 7 July 1951

On poets

. . . men wha through the ages sit,
And never move frae aff the bit,
Wha hear a Burns or Shakespeare sing,
Yet still their ain bit jingles string,
As they were worth the fashioning.

HUGH MACDIARMID (C.M. Grieve, 1892–1978),
'A Drunk Man Looks at the Thistle'

On political economy

. . . what we might call, by way of eminence, the dismal science

THOMAS CARLYLE (1795–1881), *The Nigger Question*

On an over-proud man

Too coy to flatter, and too proud to serve,
Thine be the joyless dignity to starve.

TOBIAS SMOLLETT (1721–71), 'Advice'

On the parliament building

Everyone here make big laugh with Scotland parliment. You pay Euros 600 millions for building that look like junk yard.

My cousin Jerzy in Leith pay 75 thousands for real scrapyard
and it has nice view of sea.

PAWEL PONIATOWSKI's blog, www.business.scotsman.com,
Przemysl, Poland, 2 Aug 2006

On the privatisation of the Trustee Savings Bank

Bank robbery is the word we use to describe the crime of
stealing from a bank. But what word can we use to describe the
crime of stealing a bank? Words cannot describe the crimes of
government!

JAMES A. WHYTE (1920–2005), letter to *The Scotsman*, 1985

On the public

I do not like mankind; but men, and not all of these – and fewer
women. As for respecting the race, and, above all, that fatuous
rabble of burgesses called 'the public', God save me from such
irreligion!

ROBERT LOUIS STEVENSON (1850–94), letter to Edmund Gosse

On publishers

They say that when the author was on the scaffold he said
goodbye to the ministers and reporters, and then he saw some

publishers sitting in the front row
below, and to them he did not say
goodbye. He said instead, 'I'll see
you later.'

SIR J.M. BARRIE (1860–1937),
Speech to the Aldine Club,
New York (1896)

Sir J.M Barrie

On pubs

When they become smoke-free, we'll smell the truth about a lot of pubs – the stale beer, stench from the toilets, BO, belches and breaking wind.

TOM BROWN, *Sunday Mirror*, 14 November 2004

On the Reformation

The Reformation was a kind of spiritual strychnine of which Scotland took an overdose.

WILLA MUIR (1890–1970), *Mrs Grundy in Scotland*

On respectability

The Scot . . . makes a great parade of his respectability and takes a genuine pride in it, just as a savage takes a great pride in his store clothes; but there is always the secret hankering for the loin-cloth and feathers, and sometimes it has its way.

DONALD CARSWELL, *Brother Scots* (1927)

> On Rozie o' the Cleugh
> I'll gie thee Rozie o' the Cleugh,
> I'm sure she'll please thee weel eneuch.
> Up wi' her on the bare bane dyke:
> She'll be rotten or I'll be ripe.

Anonymous, 'Hey, Wully Wine'

On Scottish football

More football later, but first let's see the goals from the Scottish Cup final.

DES LYNAM (1942–), TV sports broadcaster

On the Scottish literati

The solemn foppery, and the gross stupidity of the Scottish literati are perfectly insupportable.

GILBERT STUART (fl. C18th), letter to a London friend, 17 June 1774

On Scottish nationalism

Let's be glad that one king and one bloody frontier have gone and recognise that the world has suffered enough from men surrendering their freedoms to ideologies, nation states, religions and football-clubs.

ALAN JACKSON (1938–), 'The Knitted Claymore' in
Lines Review, June 1971

On a show-off

He doesnae juist drap a name
or set it up and say grace wi't,
he lays it oot upon his haun
and hits ye richt in the face wi't.

T.S. LAW (1916–97), 'Importance'

On smoking

Is it not both great vanitie and uncleanness, that at the table, a place of respect, of cleanlinesse, of modestie, men should not be ashamed, to sit tossing of Tobacco pipes, and puffing of the smoke of Tobacco one to another, making the filthy smoke and stink thereof, to exhale athwart the dishes, and infect the aire, when very often men that abhorre it are at their repast?

KING JAMES VI (1566–1625), *A Counterblaste to Tobacco*

On some residents of Langholm

O arselins wi' them! Whummle them again!
Coup them heels-owre-gowdy in a storm sae gundy
That mony a lang fog-theekit face I ken
'll be sooked richt doon under a cundy
In the High Street.

HUGH MACDIARMID
(C.M. Grieve, 1892–1978)

On success and failure

Still, failure, success, what is it? Whae gies a fuck. We aw live,
then we die, in quite a short space ay time n aw. That's it; end
ay fucking story.

IRVINE WELSH (1958–),
Trainspotting

On taxi-drivers

The stamp-peyin self-employed ur truly the lowest form ay
vermin oan god's earth.

IRVINE WELSH (1958–),
Trainspotting

On television in Scotland

You just have to watch the Scottish BAFTAs to want to kill
yourself.

MURIEL GRAY (1959–), interview in
Scotland on Sunday, 14 January 1996

On thiggers

Some little of the thiggers' styles I will set forth; they are
Roving-eye sons, Fly-by-night sons while yet far off.
They are Early-rising sons, who on a summer's day demand
more sun; Spyer-sons, Greedy-sons are they all.

GIOLLA COLUIM MACMHUIRICH (fl. C15th), from a poem on
thiggers (abusers of hospitality) in the *Book of the Dean of Lismore*,
translated from Gaelic

On two judges: Smith and Moseley

Smith, Mosely and Necessity
Resemble one another;
Necessity it hath no Law,
Nor Smith, nor Moseley either.

SAMUEL COLVILLE or COLVIN (1676)

On the unco guid

O ye wha are sae guid yoursel,
Sae pious and sae holy,
Ye've nought to do but mark and tell
Your neibours' fauts and folly!

ROBERT BURNS (1759–96), 'Address to the Unco Guid,
or the Rigidly Righteous'

On the un-reasoning

He who will not reason is a bigot; he who cannot is a fool;
and he who dares not, is a slave.

WILLIAM DRUMMOND (1585–1649), 'Academical Question'

On up-rooters of trees

Primitive people used to worship trees . . . if their beliefs have any foundation in truth I know some Fife farmers who must go haunted to their graves.

CHRISTOPHER RUSH, *A Twelvemonth and a Day* (1985)

On William MacGonagall

William MacGonagall was not a bad poet; still less a good bad poet. He was not a poet at all.

HUGH MACDIARMID (C.M. Grieve, 1892–1978), 'Scottish'

On women MPs

The women in the House of Commons are mostly hideous. They have no fragrance . . . cagmags, scrubheaps, old tattles.

SIR NICHOLAS FAIRBAIRN (1933–95), obituary in *The Scotsman*, February 1995, quoted in A. Cran and J. Robertson, *Dictionary of Scottish Quotations* (1996)

On youth

There is a great deal more to be said about youth, but very little in its favour. Its most attractive qualities – its only attractive qualities – are innocence and physical beauty. But these are not in themselves sources of illimitable interest.

J.M. BRIDIE (Osborne Henry Mavor, 1888–1957), *Mr Bridie's Alphabet for little Glasgow highbrows*

Parliament, politics and government

Brodie: No innocent blood in all his reign was shed.
Lillias: Save all Glencoe in one night murdered.
Brodie: He saved our country, and advanced our trade.
Lillias: Witness such product we from Darien had.

> Anonymous, imaginary dialogue between the Laird of Brodie
> and Lillias Brodie, on the death of King William II (1702),
> from J. Maidment, *Book of Scottish Pasquils* (1866)

Four and twenty blacklegs, working night and day,
Fed on eggs and bacon, getting double pay;
Helmets on their thick heads, bayonets gleaming bright,
If someone burst a sugar bag, the lot would die of fright.

> Anonymous, student magazine of 1928, quoted in
> Roy M. Pinkerton, 'Of Chambers and Communities', in
> G. Donaldson, *Four Centuries: Edinburgh University Life* (1983)

This is the savage pimp without dispute
First bought his mother for a prostitute;
Of all the miscreants ever went to hell,
This villain rampant bears away the bell.

> Anonymous, C17th,
> on the Duke of Lauderdale (1616–82),
> Secretary for Scotland

The Stuarts, antient true-born race,
We must all now give over;
We must receive into their place
The mungrells of Hanover

'A Curse on The Unionists and Revolutionaries',
from J. Maidment, *Book of Scottish Pasquils* (1866)

Our Duiks were deills, our marquesses were mad,
Our Earls were evills, our Viscounts yet more bade,
Our Lords were villains, and our Barons knaves,
Quho with our burrows did sell us for slaves

Verses on the Scottish Peers, 1706,
from J. Maidment, *Book of Scottish Pasquils* (1866)

Auld Satan cleekit him by the spaul
And stappit him in the dub o' Hell.
The foulest fiend there daurna bide him,
The damned they wadna fry beside him.
Till the bluidy Duke cam trysting thither,
And the ae fat butcher fried the ither.

Anonymous, Jacobite verse from Cromek's *Select Scottish Songs* (1810),
on Sir John Murray of Broughton, the turncoat Jacobite,
and the Duke of Cumberland

O Bute, if instead of contempt and of odium,
You wish to obtain universal eulogium,
From your breast to your gullet transfer the blue string
Our hearts are all yours from the very first swing.

Anonymous, C18th,
on the Earl of Bute (1713–92),
Prime Minister

Stick to Marx, my hearty,
Damn the Labour Party

Anonymous street song, early C20th

It's Edinburgh's thing. All your smiley, interlocking circles of power where they manicure their nails on each other's backs.

Glaswegian comment on parliament,
quoted in *The Scotsman*, 10 October 2004

The Vichy parliament.

www.siol-nan-gaidheal.com, on the Scottish parliament

London's man in Edinburgh.

www.siol-nan-gaidheal.com, on Jack McConnell, First Minister

George Galloway, MP: 'Why do people take such an instant dislike to me?' Unnamed colleague: 'It saves time.'

MATTHEW PARRIS and PHIL MASON, *Read My Lips*, 1996

All political parties die at length of swallowing their own lies.

JOHN ARBUTHNOT (1667–1735)

Andrew Bonar Law

. . . has not the brains of a Glasgow bailie

H.H. ASQUITH (1852–1928), to David Lloyd George, quoted in Frances Stevenson, *Diary*, November 1916, on Andrew Bonar Law (1858–1923), former prime minister of Britain

He pursues us with a malignant fidelity.

> ARTHUR JAMES BALFOUR (1848–1930), on an unwanted supporter,
> quoted in Winston Churchill, *Great Contemporaries* (1937)

I thought he was a young man of promise; but it appears he was a young man of promises.

> ARTHUR JAMES BALFOUR on Winston Churchill, quoted in
> Randolph Churchill, *Winston Churchill, Vol. 1* (1966)

It's like any Parish Council . . .

> TONY BLAIR (1953–), on the proposed Scottish parliament

His long lank and greasy hair made him look like an Indian squaw who had lost interest in life and had decided to let everything go . . . ended as the most popular member of the Commons . . . rather a queer ending for the apostle of 'socialism in our time'.

> COLM BROGAN, *The Glasgow Story* (1952), on James Maxton

James Maxton

No Chancellor until this has come to the House and said that because he had money available to him the rich will get the benefits and the poor will make the sacrifices.

> GORDON BROWN (1951–), quoted in *The Observer*,
> May 1988, on Norman Lamont's Budget

They can call themselves the White Heather Club if they want, they will never be the Scottish government.

TOM BROWN, *New Statesman*, January 2001, quoting a 'senior figure at Westminster' on the Scottish Executive's wish to call itself the Scottish Government; the Scottish National Party welcomed the suggested name-change, seeing it as another small step on the road to independence; Margo MacDonald MSP suggested that Scotland's Westminster parliamentarians should be renamed WMPs, pronounced 'wimps'

He was the coldest friend and the violentest enemy I ever had.

GILBERT BURNET (1643–1715), *History of His Own Time*, on the first Duke of Lauderdale, Secretary for Scotland

What force or guile could not subdue
Thro' many warlike ages,
Is wrought now by a coward few,
For hireling traitor's wages.
The English steel we could disdain,
Secure in valour's station;
But English gold has been our bane –
Such a parcel of rogues in a nation!

ROBERT BURNS (1759–96), 'Such a Parcel of Rogues in a Nation', on those Scots bribed to support the Treaty of Union, 1707

. . . a cursed old Jew, not worth his weight in cold bacon

THOMAS CARLYLE (1795–1881), on Benjamin Disraeli (1804–81), Tory Prime Minister; in Monypenny and Buckle, *The Life of Benjamin Disraeli, Earl of Beaconsfield* (1913)

Gladstone appears to me one of the contemptiblest men I ever looked on.

THOMAS CARLYLE (1795–1881), on William Ewart Gladstone (1809–98), Liberal Prime Minister

I remember, when I was a child, being taken to the celebrated Barnum's Circus, which contained an exhibition of freaks and monstrosities; but the exhibit on the programme which I most desired to see was the one described as 'The Boneless Wonder'. My parents judged that the spectacle would be too revolting and demoralising for my youthful eyes, and I have waited fifty years to see The Boneless Wonder sitting on the Treasury Bench.

WINSTON CHURCHILL (1874–1965), on Ramsay MacDonald (1866 1937), Labour and then National Government Prime Minister, in the House of Commons

We know that he has, more than any other man, the gift of compressing the largest number of words into the smallest amount of thought.

> WINSTON CHURCHILL (1874–1965), on Ramsay MacDonald (1866–1937), Labour and then National Government Prime Minister, in the House of Commons

He is too Scotch to perceive that nobody wants him, and if he saw it he is too Scotch to go.

> T.W.H. CROSLAND, *The Unspeakable Scot* (1902), on Sir Henry Campbell-Bannerman (1836–1908), leader of the Liberal Party, later prime minister

Campbell-Bannerman

> Wha the de'il hae we gotten for a king,
> But a wee, wee German lairdie!

ALLAN CUNNINGHAM (1784–1842), 'Wha The De'il Hae We Gotten for a King'; this is included on sufferance for its fame. Its author was born seventy years after George I came to the throne. Like most well-known Jacobite songs, it is post-Jacobite in origin.

He has all the qualifications for a great Liberal Prime Minister. He wears spats and he has a beautiful set of false teeth.

> R.B. CUNNINGHAME GRAHAM (1852–1936),
> on Sir Henry Campbell-Bannerman, Prime Minister

The Prime Minister is a sustained, brazen deceiver . . . I say she is a bounder, a liar, a deceiver, a cheat and a crook.

> TAM DALYELL (1932–), MP, on Mrs Margaret Thatcher,
> 29 October 1988

Socialism? These days? There's the tree that never grew. Och, a shower of shites. There's the bird that never flew.

> CAROL ANN DUFFY (1955–), 'Politico'

The late Oliver Brown . . . put it well. He said that when I won Hamilton you could feel a chill run along the Labour back benches looking for a spine to run up.

> WINNIE EWING (1929–), Nationalist politician,
> quoted in Kenneth Roy, *Conversations in a Small Country* (1989)

The Honourable Lady was once an egg, and people on both sides of this House greatly regret its fertilisation.

> SIR NICHOLAS FAIRBAIRN (1933–95), on Mrs Edwina Currie, during a
> parliamentary debate, at the time of the 1988 salmonella scare

It is fit only for the slaves who sold it.

> ANDREW FLETCHER OF SALTOUN (1655–1716), comment on Scotland
> after the Union with England in 1707, in G.W.T. Ormond,
> *Fletcher of Saltoun* (1897)

. . . an afterthought given to the most compliant minister who is not expected to do very much

> SAM GALBRAITH, former holder of the post, on the role of
> culture minister as exercised by Frank McAveety,
> *Scotland on Sunday*, 13 June 2004

He had sufficient conscience to bother him, but not enough to keep him straight.

> DAVID LLOYD GEORGE (1863–1945),
> on Ramsay MacDonald (1866–1937),
> Labour and National Government Prime Minister

A one-eyed fellow in blinkers.

> DAVID LLOYD GEORGE (1863–1945), on Lord Rosebery (1847–1929),
> Liberal Prime Minister

Gordon Brown, who, like Napoleon, or Stalin, or Hitler, aspires to come from a distant province or satellite state and take over the mother country.

> SIMON HEFFER, *The Daily Telegraph*,
> 15 January 2007

Mr Kirkwood: What about Calton Jail, that is empty?
Duchess of Atholl: If the honourable member would like to be returned as a representative of his constituency to the Calton Jail, he is quite welcome to do so.
Mr Kirkwood: I have been there before.

Hansard, 1924, quoted in Andrew Marr, *The Battle for Scotland* (1992)

On Hardie's first day at the House of Commons, the policeman at the gate took one look at the former miner, dressed in his ordinary working clothes and cloth cap, and asked suspiciously, 'Are you working here?'

'Yes,' replied Hardie.

'On the roof?'

'No,' said the new MP. 'On the floor.'

In C. FADIMAN, *The Little, Brown Book of Anecdotes*, (1985), on James Keir Hardie (1856–1915), the first Labour MP

The Scottish Tories are an extreme case of necrophilia.

CHRISTOPHER HARVIE (1944–), *Cultural Weapons*

Jean Hamilton . . . fell out on me publiklye that I could not spell nor pronounce and then told that I was Kings Advocat and had sold the King as Judas had sold his Master, that their was a Judas heir, that I had killed Earle of Montrose . . . that tho I pretended to denye the world I had it fast in my airmes.

ARCHIBALD JOHNSTON OF WARISTON (1611–63), *Diary*, June 1656

The vast majority of Scotland's elected representatives are moral and political cowards.

JAMES KELMAN (1946–), *Some Recent Attacks*

Of course us artists aren't supposed to talk about political issues, we are too idealistic, we don't have a firm enough grasp on reality . . . It's quite remarkable really the different ways whereby the state requires its artists to suck dummy tits.

JAMES KELMAN (1946–), Lecture at Glasgow School of Art, 1996

May his guts fall out.

NORMAN MACCAIG (1910–96), on a Lord Provost of Edinburgh, in Karl Miller, *Rebecca's Vest* (1993)

He is in fact a zombie. . . not really a Scotsman of course, but only a sixteenth part of one, and all his education and social affiliations are anti-Scottish. Sir Walter warned long ago that a Scotchman unscotched would become only a damned mischievous Englishman, and that is precisely what has happened in this case.

HUGH MACDIARMID (C.M. Grieve, 1892–1978), when standing as a Communist candidate against Sir Alec Douglas-Home in September 1964

All government is a monopoly of violence.

HUGH MACDIARMID (C.M. Grieve, 1892–1978), 'A Glass of Pure Water'

If I had my way
I would melt your gold payment,
Pour it into your skulls
Until it reached your boots.

IAIN LOM MACDONALD (c. 1620–c. 1707), 'Oran na Agaidh na
Aonaidh' ('Song Against the Union'), attacking those who were
bribed to support the Union with England

Margaret Thatcher is not just a perpetrator of bad policies.
She is a cultural vandal. She takes the axe of her own simplicity
to the complexities of Scottish life.

WILLIAM MCILVANNEY (1936–), Speech to the
Scottish National Party Conference, September 1987,
published in W. McIlvanney, *Surviving the Shipwreck* (1991)

. . . you have adopted the rule and course
That Judas, your own brother, followed;
great is the scandal in your country
that such a brute did grow in it . . .
You have talked unsparingly of Scotland,
and had better have kept silent;
Were you to come to the Rough Bounds
Woe to one in your case.

DUNCAN BÀN MACINTYRE (1724–1812), 'Song to John Wilkes',
from the Gaelic; Wilkes was an English politician notable
for anti-Scottish, or anti-Jacobite, sentiments

When Harold Macmillan, as Prime Minister, suddenly sacked
many of his Cabinet colleagues, the Lord Chancellor, Lord
Kilmuir, complained: 'A cook would have been given more
notice of his dismissal.'
'Ah,' said Macmillan, 'but good cooks are hard to find.'

Told to the compiler by a member of the the the Macmillan family

It puts us up there with the Nazi Reichstag and Supreme Soviet Assembly as a parliament with an instinct for banning writers. What's next? A mass burning of books which do not receive the imprimatur of the Scotia Nostra?

> JAMES MACMILLAN (1959–), on the parliamentary motion
> to repudiate the 'Clearance Denial' views of Michael Fry,
> signed among others by 'the terminally embarrassing
> Rosanna Cunningham'

A Scandinavian-style study centre for the propagation of dullness and depression.

> ROBERT MACNEIL, *The Scotsman*, 24 February 2000
> on the Scottish parliament

Annabel Goldie, one-time doughty hockey player and now maternal aunt to the eccentrics and aristocrats of the Scottish Conservative Party, took her rightful place in the leader's chair at the Scottish Parliament . . . With the reproving voice of Miss Jean Brodie and the withering, glasses-down-the-end-of-the-nose stare of James Robertson Justice, Miss Goldie was out to prove she was the equal of Jack McConnell during First Minister's Questions.

By her side sat sullen Murdo Fraser, the new deputy leader of the Scottish Tories. One Tory activist unkindly dubbed the new leadership dream team as 'Hattie Jacques and Son of Vulcan' . . . A firm, authoritative voice like Miss Goldie's must have a special resonance for some former schoolboys – at least one of the Old Etonians in the Tory ranks sat bolt upright as if woken from a daydream as soon as she started speaking.

> ROBERT MACNEIL, *The Scotsman*, 4 November 2005

Sam Galbraith, the Glaswegian minister of education and alumnus of Heidbutter High.

ROBERT MACNEIL, *The Scotsman*, 23 March 2000

I have never concealed that in my youth I was a Conservative; but never, in the depths of my igorance and degradation, was I a Liberal.

JAMES MAXTON (1885–1946), replying in the House of Commons to a member who accused him of having once been a Liberal

Sit down, man. You're a bloody tragedy.

JAMES MAXTON (1885 1946) to Ramsay MacDonald while the latter was making his last speech in parliament

British 'Parliamentary cretinism' (to use Lenin's old phrase) had found its last abiding refuge within the Scottish National Party, where sectarian infantilism seems likely to keep the old thing warm until a true Doomsday comes.

TOM NAIRN (1932–), 'The Timeless Girn', in O.D. Edwards, *A Claim of Right for Scotland* (1989)

This evil mélange of decrepit Presbyterianism and imperialist thuggery, whose spirit may be savoured by a few mornings with the Edinburgh *Scotsman* and a few evenings watching Scottish television, appears to be solidly represented in the SNP.

TOM NAIRN (1932–), *The Three Dreams of Scottish Nationalism*

No one really thinks the shade of William Wallace will re-appear at Holyrood. A lot of people do think, with appropriate despondency, that Councillor McDirge, Provost McBaffie and

Mrs McGrunge will not only be in there but could soon swamp the place.

TOM NAIRN (1932–), *After Britain 2000*

I remember the time when his life would not have been worth twopence, but I urge you to do him no physical injury. It is hard, I know, for you to tolerate him in your midst, but I pray to God that you may restrain yourselves.

FATHER A. O'BRIEN, parish priest of Shettleston, in Ian Wood, *John Wheatley*, on a Socialist parishioner, 1911

Long and lean, with the features of a kindly giraffe.

EDWARD PEARCE, *Humming Birds and Hyenas* (1985), on Donald Dewar (1937–2000), first First Minister

The Tories are looking increasingly desperate. They are an irrelevance . . . The reason we object to them is their anti-Scottish policy stances. That is why they remain the pariahs of Scottish politics.

ALEX SALMOND (1954–) MSP, SNP leader, in *The Scotsman*, 23 May 2006

A revolving door for jobs for the boys.

ALEX SALMOND (1954–), on Donald Dewar's first government team

Brown is prudent with pensioners and profligate with wars. He's out to get the big job but has forgotten the people back home.

ALEX SALMOND (1954–), on Gordon Brown (1951–)

They have been on a banana-shaped learning curve and more often than not have slid down it.

> Editorial on members of the Scottish parliament,
> *The Scotsman*, September 1999

The Right Honourable Gentleman is indebted to his memory for his jests and to his imagination for his facts.

> RICHARD BRINSLEY SHERIDAN (1751–1816),
> on Henry Dundas, the Tory government's manager
> of Scottish affairs, in the House of Commons

Medals are given to people who've done something, and so far we've done bugger all.

> TOMMY SHERIDAN MSP, on the Scottish
> parliament's commemoration medals, 1999

There is no art which one government sooner learns of another than of draining money from the pockets of the people.

> ADAM SMITH (1723–90), *The Wealth of Nations*

[Palmerston's] manner when speaking is like a man washing his hands; the Scotch members don't know what he is doing.

> SYDNEY SMITH (1771–1845) Lady Holland,
> *Memorial of the Rev. Sydney Smith* (1855)

Labour in Scotland have been launched more often than a lifeboat.

> NICOLA STURGEON MSP (1970–), August 1999

One may reasonably say that the arrangements under which Scotland was governed for a century and a quarter represented not so much a constitution as a bad joke elaborated with the careful logic of lunacy.

> Colin Walkinshaw (James M. Reid), *The Scots Tragedy* (1935)

Rearrange the following into a well-known phrase or saying – prat, little, pompous – and it will immediately be evident that it is of President Lord Sir David Steel that we treat.

> Gerald Warner, *Scotland on Sunday*, September 1999

The stark reality is that any tyrannical measure which can command the support of just 65 Holyrood knuckletrailers can be enforced upon Scotland. MSPs have no notion of statecraft: they have brought with them from the smoke-filled council chambers and trade union covens of the central belt the unreconstructed prejudices of an underclass. Power exists to be abused and these beggars on horseback intend to snap their fingers at every waiter in sight.

> Gerald Warner, *Scotland on Sunday*, 17 February 2002

. . . being briefed on politics by Brian Monteith would be like listening to a lecture on logical positivism by Peaches Geldof

> Gerald Warner, *Scotland on Sunday*, November 2005;
> Monteith resigned from the Scottish Conservative Party
> in November 2005 after accusations of disloyalty

Why are we ruled by a gang of cooncillors and fat women from social work departments?

> Gerald Warner, *Scottish Daily Mail*

Personal remarks and put-downs

Some traditional examples

Awa' an' bile yer heid.
Awa' and raffle yer onions.
Away to Banff and gether buckies.
Aebody's queer but you an' me: an' sometimes you're queer.
Does your mither ken you're oot?

He's yin o' thae etten-an'-spewed characters.
He thinks he's honey but the bees don't know.
If she was chocolate she wad eat hersel.
My wee wife's a bonny wee wife: Your wee wife's a deevil.
Shut your legs – here's
    a car comin'.

Skinny malinky lang-legs, big banana feet, went tae the pictures and couldna find a seat.

Tak' a long walk affa short pier.

Ye'll be a man before your mither.

Yer tongue wad clip cloots.

If I had a belly like yours I'd tie it to a tree and let the birds peck it.

On faces

Add 'He's got' or 'She's got' as necessary:

A face like the back o' the lum.

A face like a bashed thripny (an 'old' money threepence coin was 12-sided).

A face like a burst couch.

A face like a burst melodeon.

A face like a bag o' bruised fruit.

A face like a hen layin razors.

A face like a saft tattie.

A face like a skittery hippen (a soiled nappy/diaper).

A face like a torn scone.

A face like a wet washing.

A face like a weel-kickit ba'.

A face like a skelped arse.

A face like a weel-kept grave.

A face like a bulldog chewin' a wasp.

A face like a melted welly.

Personalities

O Allison Gross, that lives in yon tower,
The ugliest witch in the north countrie.

Anonymous, 'Allison Gross', C16th ballad

He is weil kend, John of the Syde,
A greater thief did never ride.

Anonymous lines on John Armstrong of Liddesdale,
in George MacDonald Fraser, *The Steel Bonnets* (1971)

Sir James Stewart, thou'lt hing in a string;
Sir James Stewart, knave and rogue thou art,
For thou ne'er had a true heart
To God or King:
Sir James Stewart, thou'lt hing in a string.

Anonymous Jacobite verse against
Sir James Stewart (died 1713), Lord Advocate

Here lies Durham
But Durham lies not here.

Epitaph for Mr Durham of Largo (fl. C18th), a noted exaggerator

Bodach an t-siapuinn (The Old Fellow of the Soap)

Gaelic nickname for Lord Leverhulme (1851–1925),
one-time proprietor of Lewis and Harris and soap millionaire

. . . Michael Scott, who verily knew well
The lightsome play of every magic fraud.

> DANTE ALIGHIERI (1265–1321), *The Inferno*,
> on a notable Scots 'wizard' of the Middle Ages

If he were a horse, no one would buy him: with that eye, no
one could answer for his temper.

> WALTER BAGEHOT (1826–77), *Biographical Studies*,
> on Lord Brougham (1778–1868), Lord Chancellor

David Hume ate a swinging great dinner,
And grew every day fatter and fatter;
And yet the great bulk of a sinner
Said there was neither spirit not matter.

> JAMES BEATTIE (1735–1803), 'On the Author of the
> Treatise of Human Nature'

David Hume

With the publication of his Private Papers in 1952, he committed suicide twenty-five years after his death.

> LORD BEAVERBROOK (1879–1964), on Earl Haig (1861–1928),
> British Commander-in-Chief in the First World War

He wasn't a one-to-one man in the pub . . . He might let you tug the hem of his garment once in a while, but that was all. He was an élitist, a platform man.

JOHN BELLANY (1942–), on Hugh MacDiarmid,
quoted in John McEwen, *John Bellany* (1994)

An ugly, cross-made, splay-footed, shapeless, little dumpling of a fellow.

Blackwood's Magazine, anonymous description of
Lord Macaulay (1800–59)

Lord Macaulay

The folks are green, it's oft been said,
Of that you'll find no trace:
There's seasoned wood in every head,
And brass in every face.
Look smart, and keep your eyes about,
Their tricks will make you grin;
The Barrhead coach will take you out,
The folks will take you in.

JAMIE BLUE (James McIndoe), 'Queer Folk at the Shaws' (c. 1820)

Of lordly acquaintance you boast,
And of dukes that you dined with yestreen:
An insect's an insect at most.
Though it crawl on the curls of a queen.

ROBERT BURNS (1759–96),
'The Toadeater'

That there is falsehood in his looks,
I must and will deny:
They tell their master is a knave,
And sure they do not lie.

ROBERT BURNS (1759–96), 'On Hearing It Asserted Falsehood is
Expressed in the Rev Dr Babington's Very Looks'

She's bow-hough'd, she's hen-shinn'd,
Ae limpin' leg a hand-breed shorter;
She's twisted right, she's twisted left,
To balance fair in ilka quarter.

ROBERT BURNS (1759–96),
'Willie Wastle'

This gentleman is the best judge of the value of his own life.

Reputed to have been said by Robert Burns of a wealthy merchant
who gave a sailor a shilling for rescuing him from Greenock Harbour

It was very good of God to let Carlyle and Mrs Carlyle marry
one another and so make only two people miserable instead of
four.

SAMUEL BUTLER (1835–1902),
in a letter, 1884

. . . Jeffrey! pertest of the train
whom Scotland pampers with her fiery grain!
Whatever blessing wait a genuine Scot,
In double portion swells thy glorious lot;
For thee Edina culls her evening sweets,
And showers her odours on thy candid sheets,
Whose hue and fragrance to thy work adhere –
This scents its pages, and that gilds its rear.

LORD BYRON (1788–1824), *English Bards and Scotch Reviewers*,
on Francis Jeffrey, of the *Edinburgh Review*

. . . the famous Nigger-Philanthropist, Drawing-room Christian, and busy man and Politician

THOMAS CARLYLE (1795–1881),
on William Wilberforce

A narrow, bitter, unreasonable being, eaten up with his own conceit, consumed with his own petty arrogance, and pursued from day to day, and year to year, by an unrelenting bee in his bonnet.

WINSTON CHURCHILL (1874–1965) on D.C. Thomson
during a speech in Dundee, November 1922

Silly, snobbish, lecherous, tipsy . . . he needed Johnson as an ivy needs an oak.

CYRIL CONNOLLY, *The Evening Colonnade*, 1990, on James Boswell

The face that launched a thousand sun-beds.

PHIL DIFFER, *The Herald*,
5 December 1999, on Tommy Sheridan

Madame, ye hev a dangerouss Dog.

> WILLIAM DUNBAR (c. 1460–c. 1520),
> 'On James Dog, Kepar of the Quenis Wardrop', a complaint to
> Queen Margaret about her wardrobe master.

Weill, gin they arena deid, it's time they were.

> ROBERT GARIOCH (Robert Garioch Sutherland, 1919–81),
> 'Elegy', on Edinburgh worthies of his youth

The 'heroic young queen' in question had the face, mind, manners and morals of a well-intentioned but hysterical poodle.

> LEWIS GRASSIC GIBBON (James Leslie Mitchell, 1901–35),
> *Scottish Scene*, on Mary, Queen of Scots

When one says of another man that he is the most arrogant man in the world, it is only to say he is very arrogant; but when one says it of Lord Kames, it is an absolute truth.

> DAVID HUME (1711–76), quoted in
> James Boswell *Journal of a Tour to the Hebrides*

Allan Ramsay, the poet, lived for a time in a remarkable house of octagonal shape on the Castle Hill of Edinburgh. He was very proud of the building, and regarded it has having exceptional beauty. Showing it one day to his friend Lord Elibank, the poet said his friends had told him it resembled a goose pie. To which Lord Elibank commented: 'Indeed, Allan, now that I see you in it, I think the term is very properly applied.'

GORDON IRVING, *The Wit of the Scots* (1969)

O Knox he was a bad man
he split the Scottish mind.
The one half he made cruel
and the other half unkind.

ALAN JACKSON (1938–), 'Knox'

He has an attractive voice and a highly unattractive bottom. In his concert performances he now spends more time wagging the latter than exercising the former.

CLIVE JAMES (1939–) on Rod Stewart (1945–)

. . . an old sausage, fizzing and sputtering in its own grease

> HENRY JAMES (1843–1916), on Thomas Carlyle

I smell you in the dark.

> SAMUEL JOHNSON (1709–84), to James Boswell

> Though thou're like Judas, an apostate black,
> In the resemblance thou dost one thing lack;
> When he had gotten his ill-purchased pelf,
> He went away and wisely hanged himself:
> This thou may do at last, but yet I doubt
> If thou hast any bowels to gush out.

> > CHARLES LAMB (1775–1834),
> > 'Epigram on Sir James Mackintosh' (1765–1832)

You can't know Burns unless you hate the Lockharts and all the estimable bourgeois and upper classes as he really did – the narrow-gutted pigeons . . . Oh, why doesn't Burns come to life again, and really salt them?

> D.H. LAWRENCE (1885–1930), letter to Donald Carswell,
> 1927, after reading Lockhart's *Life of Burns*

The Judas of his country . . . the bane of Scotland in general.

> GEORGE LOCKHART OF CARNWATH (1673–1731),
> *Memoirs Concerning the Affairs of Scotland,*
> on the first Earl of Stair

> Ablachs, and scrats, and dorbels o' a' kinds
> Aye'd drob me wi' their puir eel-dronin' minds,

Wee drochlin' craturs drutling their bit thochts
The dorty bodies! Feech! Nae Sassunach drings
'll daunton me.

> HUGH MACDIARMID (C.M. Grieve, 1892–1978),
> *Gairmscoile*, on some contemporary verse-writers

. . . the whole gang of high mucky-mucks, famous fatheads, old wives of both sexes, stuffed shirts, hollow men with headpieces stuffed with straw, bird-wits, lookersunder-beds, trained seals, creeping Jesuses, Scots Wha Ha'evers, village idiots, policemen, leaders of white-mouse factions and noted connoisseurs of bread and butter . . . and all the touts and toadies and lickspittles of the English Ascendancy, and their infernal womenfolk.

> HUGH MACDIARMID (C.M. Grieve, 1892–1978),
> *Lucky Poet*, on his literary and political opponents

. . . a paladin in mental fight with the presence of a Larry the Lamb

> HUGH MACDIARMID (C.M. Grieve, 1892–1978),
> *Lucky Poet*, on Edwin Muir (1887–1959)

Here's your likeness again:
a wisp-headed scowler,
without hat or wig,
without headpiece or crest,
you're plucked bald and bare;
with mange at your elbows
and the scratch-marks of itch at your arse.

> DUNCAN BÀN MACINTYRE (1724–1812), 'Song for the Tailor'

The laird's nae what you could call very intelligent. There's
naething in him except what he puts in with a spoon.

R.F. MACKENZIE, *A Search for Scotland* (1989)

Alasdair . . . if grace goes with gloom, great is the good you
have got from God.

DONNCHADH MAC AN PHEARSÙINN, from a poem in the
Book of the Dean of Lismore (early C16th) from the Gaelic

Canker'd, cursed creature, crabbed, corbit kittle,
Buntin-ars'd, beugle-back'd, bodied like a beetle;
Sarie-shitten, shell-padock, ill-shapen shoit,
Kid-bearded gennet, all alike great
Fiddle-douped, flindrikin, fart of a man,
Wa worth the, wanwordie, wanshapen wran.

SIR THOMAS MAITLAND, 'Satire upon Sir Neil Laing' (c. 1556)

The fattest hog in Epicurus' sty.

WILLIAM MASON, 'An Heroic Epistle to
Sir William Chambers', on David Hume

Lovat's head i' the pat,
Horns and a' the gither,
We'll mak brose o' that
An' gie the swine their supper.

HUGH MILLER (1802–56), *Scenes and Legends of the
North of Scotland*, quoting a local rhyme on
Lord Lovat, who was executed in 1746

In the furor which followed Boswell's *Life of Johnson*, [Lord
Monboddo (1714–99)] was asked what he thought of Boswell.

He replied, 'Before I read his book I thought he was a Gentleman who had the misfortune to be mad: I now think he is a
madman who has the misfortune not to be a Gentleman.'

In E.L. CLOYD, *James Burnett, Lord Monboddo* (1972)

He comes out of the shop
with the latest fashion from France
and the fine clothes worn on his person
yesterday with no little satisfaction
are tossed into a corner

RODERICK MORISON (c. 1656–c. 1714), Oran dho MhacLeòid Dhùn
Bheagan (Song on MacLeod of Dunvegan), the young wastrel chief

the archetypal Scotch crawler

TOM NAIRN (1932–), 'The Timeless
Girn', in O.D. Edwards, *A Claim of Right
for Scotland* (1989), on Andrew Neil

Jemmy . . . in recording the noble growlings of the Great Bear,
thought not of his own Scotch snivel.

CHRISTOPHER NORTH (John Wilson, 1785–1854),
Noctes Ambrosianae, on James Boswell

How many times do I have to flush before he goes away? Gerald
Warner. The Scottish press loves him. Sexually repressed? Can
you use a biro? You'll do! . . . Gerald? Earth is full. Go home.

GARY OTTON's Scottish Media Monitor, *ScotsGay*, March 1999

I was present in a large company at dinner, when Bruce was
talking away. Someone asked him what musical instruments

were used in Abyssinia. Bruce hesitated, not being prepared for the question, and at last said, 'I think I saw one lyre there.' George Selwyn whispered his next man, 'Yes, and there is one less since he left the country.'

Recorded of James Bruce of Kinnaird (1730–94),
author of *A Journey to the Source of the Nile*,
in John Pinkerton, *Walpoliana* (1799)

When Carlyle's thunder had been followed by his wife's sparkle, their sardonic host said in a half-soliloquy which was intended to be audible: 'As soon as that man's tongue stops, that woman's begins.'

Quoted of Samuel Rogers in Francis Espinasse,
Literary Recollections and Sketches (1893)

I have spent my entire adult life arguing for independence. He spent the first half of his political career arguing against it, and the past ten years attacking those who argue for it on the basis that we don't believe in it as much as he does.

ALEX SALMOND, letter to *The Scotsman*,
12 September 2003, on Jim Sillars

Sellar, daith has ye in his grip;
Ye needna think he'll let ye slip.
Justice ye've earned, and, by the Book,
A warm assize ye winna jouk.
The fires ye lit to gut Strathnaver,
Ye'll feel them noo – and roast forever.

Lines on Patrick Sellar, the Duke of Sutherland's factor, acquitted in court for his actions in the Sutherland Clearances, in Hamish Henderson, *The Armstrong Nose: Selected Letters of Hamish Henderson*, edited by Alec Findlay (1996)

Lord Charlemont described the expression of his mouth as imbecilic, that of his eyes as vacant, and the corpulence of his frame as befitting rather a 'turtle-eating alderman' than a philosopher.

ALASTAIR SMART, *The Life and Art of Allan Ramsay* (1952),
on David Hume

A Renaissance man, if only we'd had a renaissance.

W. GORDON SMITH, *Mr Jock* (1987), on King James IV

John Paul Jones demonstrates, better than anybody, that endearing protean quality of the Scot, to be all things to all men, providing the price is right.

W. GORDON SMITH, Mr Jock (1987), on John Paul Jones,
Scottish-born 'father' of the US Navy

The grating scribbler! whose untuned Essays
Mix the Scotch Thistle with the English Bays;
By either Phoebus preordained to ill,
The hand prescribing, or the flattering quill,
Who doubly plagues, and boasts two Arts to kill.

J.M. SMYTHE, 'One Epistle to Mr Alexander Pope',
on the doctor-poet John Arbuthnot (1667–1735)

When Barrie cam to Paradise
He gar'd the place look droller [*made*]
Sin they rigged him out in velvet breeks
And a braw new Eton collar.

WILLIAM SOUTAR (1898–1943),
on J.M. Barrie

. . . up to his death three years before, she had been living with Lord Alfred Douglas, the fatal lover of Oscar Wilde, an arrangement which I imagine would satisfy any woman's craving for birth control . . . I used to think it a pity that her mother rather than she had not thought of birth control . . . I was young and pretty; she had totally succumbed to the law of gravity.

MURIEL SPARK (1918–2006), *Curriculum Vitae*, on Marie Stopes, the Edinburgh-born pioneer of birth control

He's gone to Heaven, no doubt, but he won't like God.

ROBERT LOUIS STEVENSON (1850–94), on Matthew Arnold

There is a certain class of clever Scotsmen, who complete their education at the University of Oxford, with results not very creditable to themselves, or to the country of their origin . . . possessed with an innate flunkeyism which leads them, not merely to bow down to and humbly accept Anglian ideas and Anglicising influences; but also with these, a desire to belittle the country which gave them birth, and to sneer at Scottish ways.

T.D. WANLISS in H.J. Hanham, *Scottish Nationalism* (1969)

One day I met Gilbert Noble, who is married to Dunkie's Jock's adopted daughter. With him was Joe Maclean, who said to me, 'Do you mind when you put the paraffin on the henhouse?' Gilbert Noble was furious at him and said, 'Joe, you should have left that alane.'

He did not worry me, but I replied, 'Yes, and do you mind when you used to piss your breeks when you were a great big loon who should have known better, and the lave of the bairns in the school were scumfished with stink?'

CHRISTIAN WATT (1833–1923), *The Christian Watt Papers*

He was so monstrously ill-favoured as to possess some of the attractiveness of a gargoyle. He had neither dignity, nor what a Roman would have called gravity. As Lord Chancellor he distinguished himself by belching from the Woolsack.

ESMÉ WINGFIELD STRATFORD (1882–1971) on
Lord Brougham (1778–1868),
Lord Chancellor of Great Britain

With an expression half-bovine and half-sheeplike he stares out of the screen in such a way as to leave us all uncertain whether he wants to cut our throats or lick our boots.

PEREGRINE WORSTHORNE (1923–), in Jonathon Green,
Dictionary of Insults (1995), on Andrew Neil

Places

Oh, — is a dirty hole,
A kirk without a steeple,
A midden heap at every door,
And damned uncivil people.

> Traditional rhyme of abuse to the next town;
> supply the place of your choice

Aberdeen . . . a thin-lipped peasant woman who has borne eleven and buried nine . . . Union Street has as much warmth in its face as a dowager duchess asked to contribute to the Red International Relief.

> LEWIS GRASSIC GIBBON (James Leslie Mitchell, 1901–35), *Scottish Scene*

No jokes of any kind are understood here, I have not made one for two months, and if I feel one coming I shall bite my tongue.

> JAMES CLERK MAXWELL (1831–79), on being elected to the
> Chair of Mathematics at Marischal College, Aberdeen

It was only in Aberdeen that I saw . . . the kind of tartan tight-fistedness that made me think of the average Aberdonian as a person who would gladly pick a penny out of a dunghill with his teeth.

> PAUL THEROUX, *A Kingdom by the Sea* (1983)

This grim, grey, sea-beaten hole.

> ROBERT LOUIS STEVENSON (1850–94),
> letter to his mother, 1868, on Anstruther

Crianlarich is the most signposted nowhere on the planet.

> JIM CRUMLEY (1947–), *Gulfs of Blue Air*

If Dingwall was in its ordinary state, it must be an excellent place for sleeping away a life in.

> LORD COCKBURN (1779–1854), *Circuit Journeys*

Dumfries. . . a blowsy, overgrown country town.

> EDWIN MUIR (1887–1959), *Scottish Journey*

The gap on the map.

> DAVID MUNDELL MSP, 21 March 2000,
> referring to how Dumfries and Galloway is seen from outside

Dundee, the palace of Scottish blackguardism, unless perhaps Paisley be entitled to contest this honour with it.

> LORD COCKBURN (1779–1854), *Circuit Journeys*

Dundee, certainly now, and for many years past, the most blackguard place in Scotland . . . a sink of atrocity . . . A Dundee criminal, especially if a lady, may be known, without any evidence about character, by the intensity of the crime, the audacious bar air, and the parting curses.

> LORD COCKBURN (1779–1854), *Circuit Journeys*

Dundee, a frowsy fisherwife given to gin and infanticide.

LEWIS GRASSIC GIBBON (James Leslie Mitchell, 1901–35), *Scottish Scene*

What bloody shits the Dundeans must be.

T.E. LAWRENCE, letter to Sir Edward Marsh, November 1922; the
Dundonians had failed to re-elect Winston Churchill as their MP

Dundee . . . As men have made it, it stands today perhaps the
completest monument in the country of human folly, avarice
and selfishness.

FIONN MACCOLLA (T.D. Macdonald, 1906–75),
in George Scott-Moncrieff, *Scottish Country* (1936)

The town is ill-built and is dirty beside,
For with water it's scantily, badly supplied . . .
And abounds so in smells that a stranger supposes
The people are very different in noses.

THOMAS STUART, *Dundee* (1815)

Dumpdee

Rude name for Dundee

Polomint City

East Kilbride, famous for its many roundabouts

this accursed, stinking, reeky mass of stones and lime and dung

THOMAS CARLYLE (1795–1881), letter to his brother John,
February 1821, on Edinburgh

Your burgh of beggaris is ane nest,
To shout the swengouris will nocht rest,
All honest folk they do molest
So piteously they cry and rame.

WILLIAM DUNBAR (c. 1460–c. 1520), 'Satire on Edinburgh'

Over five hundred years later, the Edinburgh City Council was still trying to expel beggars from the city centre:

> . . . this sad old city – you see her pinioned by her judges and preyed on by their wig-lice, that countless vermin of law-yerlings, swollen and small. You see her left in squalor by her shopkeepers, the bawbee-worshipping bailie-bodies, and pushioned by her doctors; you hear her dulled by the blithers of her politicians and deived by the skreigh of the newsboy-caddies who squabble at their heels, and you know how she has been paralysed by the piffle of her professors, more than half-doited or driven into alter-nate hidebound or hysteric nightmares by every chilly dogmatism, every flaring hell-blast imagined by three cen-turies and more of diabologic Divines.

> SIR PATRICK GEDDES (1854–1932), letter to
> R.B. Cunninghame Graham (August 1909), in
> P. Boardman, *The Worlds of Patrick Geddes* (1978)

Edinburgh . . . a disappointed spinster with a hare-lip and inhibitions.

LEWIS GRASSIC GIBBON (James Leslie Mitchell, 1901–35), *Scottish Scene*

If the world comes to an end, Edinburgh will never notice.

JO GRIMOND (1913–96), interview in *The Scotsman*, 27 October 1979

As every schoolboy knows, Edinburgh is redolent with history, which in the case of Scotland consists mainly of people knifing one another or blowing up one another's bedrooms.

CLIFF HANLEY (1922–99)

Most of the denizens wheeze, snuffle and exhale a sort of snozzling whnoff, whnoff, apparently through a hydrophile sponge.

EZRA POUND (1885–1972), in Hugh MacDiarmid,
Lucky Poet (1943), on Edinburgh

The saturnine Heart of Midlothian, never mine.

MURIEL SPARK (1918–2006), on Edinburgh

I mortally detest and abhor this place, and everybody in it. Never was there a city where there was so much pretension to knowledge, that had so little of it.

GILBERT STUART (fl. C18th), letter to a London friend,
17 June 1774, on Edinburgh

I do wonder that so brave a prince as King James should be born in so stinking a town as Edinburgh in lousy Scotland.

SIR ANTHONY WELDON,
A Perfect Guide to the People and Country of Scotland (1617)

Fish guts and stinkin' herrin
Are bread and milk for an Eyemouth bairn

Old rhyme

The cavemen

Largs boys' name for the inhabitants of Fairlie

Fort Augustus
Did disgust us,
And Fort William did the same.
At Letterfinlay
We fared thinly;
At Ballachulish
We looked foolish,
Wondering why we thither came

WILLIAM WORDSWORTH (1770–1850), quoted in Robert Southey,
Journal of a Tour in Scotland in 1819

Girvan – a cauld, cauld place. Naebuddy o' ony consequence
was ever born here.

'ROBIN ROSS', in *The Chiel*, January 1885,
quoted in William Donaldson, *The Language of the People* (1989)

Glasgow is not for me.
I do not see the need for such a crowd.

Anonymous Gaelic poet, quoted in Alasdair Maclean,
Night Falls on Ardnamurchan (1989)

'Heaven seems vera little improvement on Glesga,' a Glasgow man is said to have murmured, after death, to a friend who had predeceased him. 'Man, this is no heaven,' the other replied.

Traditional

Glasgow, that damned sprawling evil town.

G.S. FRASER (1915–80), *Meditation of a Patriot*

Glasgow . . . the vomit of a cataleptic commercialism.

LEWIS GRASSIC GIBBON (James Leslie Mitchell, 1901–35),
The Thirteenth Disciple

Then suddenly the sun was snuffed
Behind a sooty cloud,
And night let fall on Glasgow Green
Its sulphur-stinking shroud.

IAIN HAMILTON (1920–86), 'News of the World'

A town with guts – you see some on the pavement.

FORBES MASSON (1964–) and ALAN CUMMING (1965–), 'Glasgow Song'

' . . . all the wise men in Glasgow come from the East – that's to say, they come from Edinburgh.'
'Yes, and the wiser they are, the quicker they come.'

NEIL MUNRO (1864–1930), *Erchie, My Droll Friend*

One day, when I was taking tea with a well-known Scottish divine in Glasgow, the conversation turned on Edinburgh, its charm, its menace, its appeal. Suddenly my companion leant forward over the table, a strange gleam in his eyes. 'They say there are more amateur tarts in Edinburgh than anywhere else,' he said, with a grave intensity.

GEORGE MALCOLM THOMSON, *The Re-Discovery of Scotland* (1928)

Alas, my native place! That Goddess of dullness has strewed on it all her poppies.

JANE WELSH CARLYLE (1801–66),
letter to Eliza Stoddart, on Haddington

Hamilton is notoriously a dull place; if a joke finds its way into our neighbourhood, it is looked upon with as much surprise as a comet would be.

Hamilton Hedgehog, October 1856

There's nothing here but Hielan' pride
And Hielan' scab and hunger;
If Providence has sent me here,
'Twas surely in an anger.

ROBERT BURNS (1759–96), 'Epigram on the Inn at Inveraray'

Inverkip is so rough they put a date-stamp on your head when they mug you so they don't do you twice in the one day.

CHIC MURRAY (1919–85), quoted in A. Yule,
The Chic Murray Bumper Fun Book (1991)

It's a shame over there –
So many Lowlanders in Inverness;
Even if there weren't so many,
I wouldn't have missed a few.

Comment on the capital of the Highlands, from the Gaelic

Glasgow has been a great home for the people of Inverness, who used to come down with the hay-seed in their boots and the heather sticking out of their ears.

JAMES MAXTON (1885–1946), in G. McAllister, *James Maxton: Portrait of a Rebel* (1935), to the MP for Inverness, in the House of Commons, 1934

Cumbernauld in a kilt.

TOM MORTON, on Inverness

Dolphinsludge.

TOM MORTON's name for Inverness

If justice were down to the inhabitants of Inverness, in twenty years' time there would be no one left there but the Provost and the hang-man.

JOHN TELFORD (d. 1807), in L.T.C. Rolt, *Thomas Telford* (1958)

Was there e'er sic a parish, a parish, a parish, a parish,
Was there e'er sic a parish as that o' Kinkell?
They've stickit the minister, hanged the precentor,
Dung doun the steeple, and drucken the bell.

Anonymous

You cut your finger and by the time news gets to the end of the road it's become an amputation.

Local resident, on Kirkcudbright, in *The Scotsman*, September 1999

. . . I could see the lights of Kirkwall twinkling across the water, miles to the south-east. 'Ah,' I would think to myself, 'there's that Babylon of a place, full of distraction and debauchery.'

WILL SELF (1961–), *The Rousay Effect*

What's Motherwell famous for?
Coal and steel.
And what's Hamilton famous for?
Stealin' coal.

One-time Motherwell saying

Musselburgh was a burgh
When Edinburgh was nane;
And Musselburgh will be a burgh
When Edinburgh is gane.

Traditional Musselburgh rhyme

At Oban of discomfort one is sure;
Little the difference whether rich or poor,

ARTHUR HUGH CLOUGH (1819–61),
Mari Magno, The Lawyer's Second Tale

Words cannot express how horrible Oban is . . . tacky beyond belief, full of disgusting shops selling Highland dancer dolls.

TOM MORTON, *Spirit of Adventure* (1985)

This bloody town's a bloody cuss,
No bloody train, no bloody bus,
And no-one cares for bloody us,
In bloody Orkney . . .

No bloody sports, no bloody games,
No bloody fun; the bloody dames
Won't even give their bloody names,
In bloody Orkney.

HAMISH BLAIR, 'Bloody Orkney', from Arnold Silcock,
Verse and Worse (1952); composed by a
serviceman during World War II

A Paisley screwdriver.

Traditional Glaswegian definition of a hammer

As quiet as the grave . . . or even Peebles.

SIR WALTER SCOTT (1771–1832)

Oh Rhynie is a cauld place,
It doesna suit a Lowland loon!
And Rhynie is a cauld clay hole,
It is na like my father's toun.

Anonymous, 'Linten Lowren'

St Monans. . . has been quaintly taken over, like many such, by
functionless foreigners . . . their seaside homes have been
prettified by the National Trust, shot right up out of the price
range of local buyers, inhabited briefly by effete antique
dealers and fifth-rate television personalities . . .

CHRISTOPHER RUSH, *A Twelvemonth and a Day* (1985)

Stonehaven . . . home of the poverty toffs, folks said, where you
might live in sin as much as you pleased but were damned to
hell if you hadn't a white sark.

LEWIS GRASSIC GIBBON (James Leslie Mitchell, 1901–35), *Cloud Howe*

Stornoway is a town distinguished by what Shakespeare described as 'a very ancient and fish-like smell'.

ALASDAIR ALPIN MACGREGOR, *The Western Isles* (1949)

Wick is . . . the meanest of men's towns, set on what is surely the baldest of God's bays.

ROBERT LOUIS STEVENSON (1850–94), letter to his mother, 1868

Repartee

Reporter at door: 'Sir James Barrie, I presume?'
Sir James Barrie: 'You do.' (closes door)

Attibuted

A Glasgow carter, needing someone to hold his horse for a moment, asked a pompous-looking gent who happened to be passing.

'My man,' said the pompous gent, 'do you realise that I am a Bailie of this city?'

'Even if you are,' said the carter, 'surely ye widnae steal my horse.'

Traditional

A prematurely white-haired man was walking down a path in a Highland glen, when he saw two girls coming towards him. As they passed, one murmured to the other:

'Snow has come early to the hills this year.'

Quick as a flash, the man replied:

'And the young cows are down in the glen already.'

From the Gaelic, traditional

At a ceilidh in the north, the Fear an Tighe rose to introduce the next performer.

'Now Miss Jeannie MacLeod will give us a song,' he said.

'She's a wee whore,' came a voice from the back of the hall.

'Nevertheless,' said the Fear an Tighe, 'she will now give us a song.'

FROM NIGEL REES, *The Guinness Dictionary of Jokes* (1995)

John Knox had a daughter, who married a prominent Presbyterian minister, John Welch. Welch was exiled to France, and, when he was very ill, his wife came to James's court to plead for him to be allowed back to Scotland . . . his majesty asked her, who was her father. She replied, 'Mr Knox.' 'Knox and Welch,' exclaimed he, 'the devil never made such a match as that.' 'It's right like, sir,' she said, 'for we never speired his advice.' . . . She again urged her request that he would give her husband his native air. 'Give him his native air,' replied the king, 'Give him the devil,' a morsel which James had often in his mouth. 'Give that to your hungry courtiers,' said she, offended at his profaneness. He told her at last, that if she would persuade her husband to submit to the bishops, he would allow him to return to Scotland. Mrs Welch, lifting up her apron, and holding it towards the king, replied, in the true spirit of her father, 'Please your majesty, I'd rather keep his head there.'

In DAVID ROSS, *From Scenes Like These* (2000)

James Gillespie, founder of the school that bears his name, made his money out of snuff-dealing. When first he became rich enough to buy a carriage, he asked Thomas Erskine to suggest a motto to go with his initials on the door.

After an instant's thought, Erskine came up with this:
'Wha wad hae thocht it,
That noses had bocht it?'

Traditional

... the Empress found some intellectual diversion in the island. In conversation with the wife of a Caledonian named Argentocoxus, after the treaty had been concluded, Julia had joked with her about the sexual customs of her people, referring to their women's freedom in having sexual intercourse with men. The Caledonian woman showed a biting humour in her reply: 'We fulfil the demands of nature in a much better way than you Roman women. We have intercourse openly with the best men – you allow yourselves to be seduced in secret by the worst of men.'

DIO CASSIUS (c. 150–c. 235), in Anthony Birley,
Septimius Severus: The African Emperor (1971),
on Severus's invasion of Caledonia, AD 208–09

On his return from the House of Lords to the Tower, an old woman, not very well favoured, had pressed through the crowd and screamed in at the window of the coach, 'You'll get that nasty head of yours chopped off, you ugly old Scotch dog,' to which he answered, 'I believe I shall, you ugly old English bitch.'

JOHN HILL BURTON, Life of Simon Lord Lovat (1847),
on the trial and execution of Lord Lovat in 1747

Don't tell me how to do my job, do I go to your job and tell you how to sweep up?

BILLY CONNOLLY (1942–), to a heckler

The medieval scholar John Scotus (c. 810–c. 877) was a member of Charlemagne's court at Aix-la-Chapelle. On day, as he was sitting opposite the king at meal-time, Charlemagne inquired of him, 'What is there between Sottum and Scottum (that is, what difference between a fool and a Scot). The Scot's legendary reply was, 'The width of this table, Sire.'

Adapted from ARNOLD FLEMING,
The Medieval Scots Scholar in France (1952)

At a country house party, the guests were having breakfast. On the sideboard was a new patent apparatus for boiling eggs. One lady, whose garrulous conversation had already irritated another guest, was standing by him as she tried to make sense of the egg boiler. In her agitation she dropped the egg. 'Oh, I've dropped it,' she cried. 'What shall I do?' 'The usual thing,' observed the other guest, 'is to cackle.'

JOHN GILLESPIE, *Humours of Scottish Life* (1904)

Jeffrey, when addressing a jury in a certain trial, had occasion to speak freely of a military officer who was a witness in the case. Having frequently described him as 'this soldier', the witness, who was present, could not restrain himself, but started up, calling out – 'Don't call me a soldier, sir; I am an officer.'

'Well, gentlemen of the jury,' proceeded Mr Jeffrey, 'this officer, who, according to his own statement, is no soldier, was the whole cause of the whole disturbance.'

ALEXANDER HISLOP, *The Book of Scottish Anecdote* (1883),
of Francis Jeffrey

'How had you the audacity, John,' said a Scottish laird to his servant, 'to go and tell some people that I was a mean fellow, and no gentleman?'

'Na, na, sir,' was the candid answer, 'you'll no catch me at the likes o' that. I aye keep my thoughts to mysel'.'

ALEXANDER HISLOP, *The Book of Scottish Anecdote* (1883)

'Is't a laddie or a lassie?' said the gardener. 'A laddie,' said the maid. 'Weel,' says he, 'I'm glad o' that, for there's ower many women in the world.' 'Hech, man,' said Jess, 'div ye no ken there's aye maist sawn o' the best crap?'

DEAN E.B. RAMSAY (1793–1872),
Reminiscences of Scottish Life and Character

. . . it appeared that Johnson no sooner saw Smith than he attacked him for some point of his famous letter on the death of Hume. 'What did Johnson say?' was the universal enquiry. 'Why, he said,' replied Smith, with the deepest expression of resentment, 'he said, you lie! 'And what did you reply?' 'I said, you are the son of a —.' On such terms did these two great moralists meet and part.

SIR WALTER SCOTT (1771–1832), in *The Life of Samuel Johnson LLD*, edited by J.W. Croker, on the meeting in Glasgow between Adam Smith and Samuel Johnson; the truth of the account has been doubted

Gilleasbuig Aotrom ('Light-headed Archie') was a familiar figure on Skye in the nineteenth century. One day he turned up at a cattle fair at Sligachan. It was cold and wet, and the small inn was packed full of the island gentry and cattle dealers from the mainland, while the crofters shivered outside. Archie pushed his way into the crowded tap-room, and was greeted by one of the lairds, MacKinnon of Corrie.

'Well, Archie, and where have you come from?'

'From Hell,' was the answer.

'Oh, that's a bad place to come from,' said Corrie. 'And what are they all doing there?'

'Just what exactly what they are doing here,' said Archie. 'The gentry is after filling the whole place and there is no room for the poor folk.'

Traditional

Reporter: 'Gordon, can we have a quick word please?'
Gordon Strachan: 'Velocity' [walks off].

On www.foxestalk.co.uk

She was beautifully attired in cream silk; the heavy piping and large buttons of her dress were covered in a fine check Fraser tartan. I decided 'Now I shall let you have it, I will take the wind out of your sails.' I asked what she thought she was. He replied that one must maintain standards; I told them they would be in a bonny mess if the poor disappeared overnight, and 'it will be a bad day for you when they decide to maintain standards.' He said, 'This is a democracy, with reasonable opportunity for all;' I said, 'That is the biggest load of dirt since the dung cart went round the Broch gathering the dry closets yesterday.' He was excited and started to habber.

'Please do not talk such vulgarity in the presence of my wife.'
I said to the wifie, 'As for you, madam, your heart is as cold as
your backside is reputed to be.'

CHRISTIAN WATT (1833–1923), *The Christian Watt Papers*, edited by
David Fraser, on talking to Lord and Lady Lovat, around 1850; the
local nickname for Lady Lovat was Lady Cauldock (cold bum)
because she found the Buchan climate chilly and even in summer
was reputed to wear two pairs of flannel drawers

Dr Taylor, the oculist, was one evening supping at William,
Earl of Dumfries's, at Edinburgh. He harangued with his usual
fluency and impudence, and boasted that he knew the
thoughts of everybody by looking at their eyes. The first Lady
Dumfries, who was hurt with his behaviour, asked him with a
smile of contempt, 'Pray, sir, do you know what I am thinking?'

'Yes, madam,' said he.

'Then,' replied the countess, 'It's very safe, for I am sure you
will not repeat it.'

ALEXANDER WEBSTER (1707–84), quoted in Charles Rogers,
Boswelliana (1874)

Schools, universities and scholars

Mr Rhind is very kind,
He goes to Kirk on Sunday.
He prays to God to give him strength
To skelp the bairns on Monday.

Traditional, on a village dominie

Spanner, screwer, lever

Unofficial motto ascribed to the Royal College of Science &
Technology, Glasgow, now the University of Strathclyde

A set o' dull, conceited hashes
confude their brains in college-classes,
They gang in stirks, and come out asses,
Plain truth to speak.

ROBERT BURNS (1759–96), 'Epistle to J. Lapraik'

I can only assume he over-celebrated – although obviously not on whisky – when he penned this tripe.

His ignorance of modern Scotland is so vast as to be hilarious. Is this really the standard of academic analysis at Harvard?

Professor Tom Devine of Edinburgh University on comments
made about modern Scotland by Professor Niall Ferguson at
Harvard University, January 2007

A kep and goun – what dae they maitter?
A kep and bells wad suit him better.

Robert Garioch (Robert Garioch Sutherland, 1909–81),
'Garioch's response Til George Buchanan'

Professor Blackie of Edinburgh University had to absent himself from his Greek lectures one day. He wrote on the blackboard in his lecture-room: 'Professor Blackie regrets that he cannot meet his classes on Thursday.' A waggish student rubbed out the 'c' of classes. Blackie, happening to notice this, also rubbed out the 'l'.

John Gillespie, *The Humours of Scottish Life* (1904)

If you should bid me count the lies of Hector's History, I might as well assay to sum the stars or waves of the sea.

John Leland on Hector Boece's *Scotorum Historiae* (1527)

You can't expect a boy to be vicious until he's been to a really good school.

> SAKI (H.H. Munro, 1870–1916) *Reginald in Russia*

He has been known to have lectured for the hour before reaching the subject of the lecture

> J.J. THOMSON, *Recollections and Reflections*,
> on Lord Kelvin (1824–1907); Kelvin was
> not a good lecturer, and his classes were
> said to resemble noisy political meetings

When Kelvin . . . went off to lay the Atlantic cable, his place was taken by a Mr Day, much inferior in scientific genius, but much superior as a teacher. Just before the great man came back, burdened with celebrity and a brand-new knighthood, a student wrote on the blackboard: 'Work while the Day liveth, for the Knight cometh wherein no man may work.'

> COLM BROGAN, *The Glasgow Story* (1952)

Scottish historiography has been for too long bogged down in a preoccupation with the myriad aspects of the Labour movement and associated areas of working-class history, to the exclusion of wider themes left virtually untouched. Short of an actual census of head lice among the children of handloom weavers in the nineteenth century, no detail of proletarian experience has been left unexplored.

> GERALD WARNER, *The Scottish Tory Party* (1988)

You could go tae University?
 – Whit fir?
Geoff had to think for a while. He had recently graduated with a degree in English Literature and was on the dole. So were most of his fellow-graduates.
 – It's a good social life, he said.

IRVINE WELSH (1958–), *Trainspotting*

... written for mentally retarded four-year-olds

KENNETH WHITE, *On Scottish Ground* (1998),
on Hume Brown's *Short History of Scotland*

I was genuinely surprised to find Alex Salmond being daft enough to put out a press release welcoming the conversion to independence of this 'historian of note' – which is a bit like describing Dr Harold Shipman as 'a physician of note'. Achieving infamy may make you 'of note' – but it doesn't mean your diagnosis of anything should be trusted.

BRIAN WILSON, *Scotland on Sunday*, 8 October 2006, on the
historian Michael Fry's espousal of Scottish Nationalism

Scotland, as seen by others

Some are of Opinion, that, when the Devil showed our Saviour the Kingdoms of the Earth, he laid his thumb upon Scotland, and that for a twofold reason: First, Because it was not like to be any Temptation, Next, Being Part of his Mother's Jointure, he could not dispose of it during her Life.

Anonymous, *Scotland Observed* (1701)

> I wondered not, when I was told
> The venal Scot his country sold,
> I rather very much admire
> How he could ever find a buyer.

Anonymous, in Nicholson, *Select Collection of Poems* (1780)

A man does well to rid himself of a turd.

Remark ascribed to King Edward I of England (1239–1307), on leaving Scotland after the Battle of Falkirk, 1298

I look upon Scotland as part of the British Empire, as it were, and when I was a kid I used to look at all the pink on the map and say, 'Isn't that marvellous! We own all that.'

JIMMY HILL, English football commentator, quoted in Roddy Forsyth, *The Only Game* (1990)

Dr Johnson: Sir, it is a very vile country.

Mr S— : Well, Sir, God made it.

Dr Johnson: Certainly He did, but we must remember He made it for Scotchmen; and comparisons are odious, Mr S—, but God made Hell.

> SAMUEL JOHNSON (1709–84), recorded in James Boswell,
> *The Life of Samuel Johnson LLD* (1791)

. . . the noblest prospect which a Scotchman ever sees, is the high road that leads him to England

> SAMUEL JOHNSON (1709–84), recorded in James Boswell,
> *The Life of Samuel Johnson LLD* (1791)

Scotland . . . whose wrinkled surface derives its original from the chaos . . . The country is full of lakes and loughs, and they well stockt with islands, so that a map thereof, looks like a pillory coat bespattered all over with dirt and rotten eggs.

> THOMAS KIRKE,
> *A Modern Account of Scotland by an English Gentleman* (1679)

This ambassador of the paipis . . . thocht it ane great mervell that sic ane thing suld be in Scotland considerand that it was bot the erse of the warld . . .

> ROBERT LINDSAY OF PITSCOTTIE (c. 1532–80),
> *The Historie and Chronicles of Scotland*, on the papal
> ambassador's reaction to the entertainment laid on by the
> Earl of Atholl for King James V in 1531

. . . a dark land overrun by homosexuals

> PAT ROBERTSON, US evangelist and financier, 1999

That garret of the earth – the knuckle-end of England – that land of Calvin, oat-cakes and sulphur.

> SYDNEY SMITH (1771–1845), in Lady Holland,
> *A Memoir of the Rev. Sydney Smith* (1855)

The air might be wholesome but for the stinking people that inhabit it; the ground might be fruitful had they the wit to manure it.

> SIR ANTHONY WELDON,
> *A Perfect Description of the People and Country of Scotland* (1617)

Scots, as seen by others

God send the land deliverance
Frae every reiving, riding Scot;
We'll sune hae neither cow nor ewe,
We'll sune hae neither staig nor stot.

Anonymous, 'The Death of Parcy Reed'

. . . there are no finer Gentlemen in the World, than that
Nation can justly boast of; but then they are such as have
travelled, and are indebted to other Countries for those
Accomplishments that render them so esteemed, their own
affording only Pedantry, Poverty, Brutality, and Hypocrisy.

Anonymous, *Scotland Characterised* (1701)

See how they press to cross the Tweed,
And strain their limbs with eager speed!
While Scotland from her fertile shore
Cries, On my sons, return no more.
Hither they haste with willing mind,
Nor cast one longing look behind.

Anonymous English verse, C18th

What is a Scot but an uninspired Irishman?

Anonymous, in Forsyth Hardy, *John Grierson's Scotland* (1979)

I have been greatly disgusted with the appearance of the brave Highlanders. They strike me as stupid, dirty, ignorant and barbarous. Their mode of life is not different from that of African negroes. Their huts are floorless except for earth, and they all live together in them like pigs; there are no chimneys, hardly any windows; no conveniences of life of any sort.

HENRY ADAMS, American visitor, in a letter to C.F. Adams, 1863

. . . the Scots are not industrious . . . They spend all their time in wars, and when there is no war they fight with one another.

DON PEDRO DE AYALA, Spanish Ambassador to King James IV, official report, July 1498

. . . of the Scots he said that they were ugly but goodnatured . . . 'They are kind, but so boring that the Lord preserve them.'

T. RATCLIFFE BARNET, on Frederic Chopin's stay in Scotland, *Scottish Pilgrimage in the Land of Lost Content* (1949)

The devellysche dysposicion of a Scottis man, not to love nor favour an Englis man . . . Trust yow no Skott.

ANDREW BOORDE, English agent, letter to Thomas Cromwell, 1536

> Then thousand schemes of petulance and pride
> Despatch her scheming children far and wide:
> Some east, some west, some everywhere but north,
> In quest of lawless gain they issue forth.

LORD BYRON (1788–1824), 'The Curse of Minerva'

Had Cain been Scot, God would have chang'd his doom;
Not forc'd him wander, but confin'd him home.

J. CLEVELAND, *Poems* (1647)

Hadrian had the excellent sense to build a wall for the purpose of keeping the Scotch out of England.

> T.W.H. CROSLAND, *The Unspeakable Scot* (1902)

A Scotchman does certainly make one feel that underneath his greasy and obviously imperfect civilisation the hairy simian sits and gibbers.

> T.W.H. CROSLAND, *The Unspeakable Scot* (1902)

If without serious inconvenience to yourself you can manage to remain at home, please do.

> T.W.H. CROSLAND, *The Unspeakable Scot* (1902) Item 10 of 'Advice to young Scots planning a career in England'

They are all gentlemen and insolent to the last degree. But certainly the absurdity is ridiculous to see a man in his mountain habit, armed with a broad sword, target, pistol or perhaps two, in his girdle a dagger, and a staff, walking down the street as upright and haughty as if he were a lord . . . and withal driving a cow.

> DANIEL DEFOE (1660–1731), in Maurice Lindsay, *The Discovery of Scotland* (1964)

A hardened, refractory people.

> DANIEL DEFOE (1660–1731), in Maurice Lindsay, *The Discovery of Scotland* (1964)

Treacherous Scotland, to no interest true.

> JOHN DRYDEN (1631–1700)

subsidy junkies

> *London Evening Standard*, 1987, quoted in Maurice Smith,
> *Paper Lions: the Scottish Press and National Identity* (1994)

If the Scots knew enough to go indoors when it rained, they would never get any exercise.

SIMEON FORD (1855–1933), *My Trip to Scotland*, an American visitor

The foul hordes of Scots and Picts like dark throngs of worms . . . a set of bloody freebooters, with more hair on their thievish faces than clothes to cover their nakedness.

> GILDAS (c. 493–570), 'De Excidio et Conquestu Britanniae',
> on the Picts, from Latin

Among ourselves, the Scotch, as a nation, are particularly disagreeable. They hate every appearance of comfort them- selves and refuse it to others. Their climate, their religion and their habits are equally averse to pleasure.

Their manners are either distinguished by a fawning syco-
phance (to gain their own ends, and conceal their natural
defects), that makes one sick; or by a morose, unbending
callousness, that makes one shudder.

WILLIAM HAZLITT (1778–1830), *Essays*

. . . we know they can remedy their poverty when they set
about it. No one is sorry for them.

WILLIAM HAZLITT (1778–1830), *Essays*

. . . when they smile, I feel an involuntary emotion to guard
myself against mischief

'JUNIUS', *Letters* (1770)

There was very little amusement in the room but a Scotchman
to hate . . . At Taylor's, too, there was a Scotchman – not quite
so bad for he was as clean as he could get himself.

JOHN KEATS (1795–1821), *Letters*

The people are proud, arrogant, vain-glorious boasters,
bloody, barbarous and inhuman butchers. Couzenage and
theft is in perfection among them, and they are perfect English
haters, they show their pride in exalting themselves, and
depressing their neighbours.

THOMAS KIRKE, *A Modern Account of Scotland
by an English Gentleman* (1679)

The tediousness of these people is certainly provoking. I
wonder if they ever tire one another! In my early life I had
a passionate fondness for the poetry of Burns. I have sometimes

foolishly hoped to ingratiate myself with his countrymen by expressing it. But I have always found that a true Scot resents your admiration of his compatriot, even more than he would your contempt of him. The latter he imputes to your 'imperfect acquaintance with many of the words which he uses;' and the same objection makes it a presumption in you to suppose that you can admire him.

CHARLES LAMB (1775–1834), 'An Imperfect Acquaintance',
in *Essays of Elia*

Among the Highlanders generally, to rob was thought at least as honourable an employment as to cultivate the soil.

LORD MACAULAY (1800–59), *History of England*

I have some good news and bad news about the English-hating Scots. The good news is that they are dying sooner than the rest of us.

The Office of National Statistics reveals that Glaswegians especially are going early.

The Government office says that thanks to a lifelong diet of misery, cynicism, fried ma arse bars and tins of syrupy beer, Glaswegians are turning in their sporrans at 70 years old, compared to the UK average of 76 . . .

The faster we accept that Scotland and England are two nations divided by a common language, the better.

My solution is simple. Build Hadrian's Wall another hundred foot higher and start airlifting in parcels of ma arse bars.

KELVIN MACKENZIE, *The Sun* (English edition only), 22 June 2006

these tartan tosspots

KELVIN MACKENZIE, *The Sun* (English edition only), 16 November 2006

No McTavish
Was ever lavish.

OGDEN NASH (1902–71)

I am glad to see you make a point of calling them 'Scotchmen'
not 'Scotsmen' as they like to be called. I find this a good easy
way of annoying them.

GEORGE ORWELL (Eric Blair, 1903–50), Letter to Anthony Powell,
1936, quoted in Christopher Harvie, *Travelling Scot* (1999)

Athenians, indeed! where is your theatre? who among you has
written a comedy? where is your Attic salt? which of you can
tell who was Jupiter's great-grandfather? . . . you know nothing
that the Athenians thought worth knowing, and dare not show
your faces before the civilised world in the practice of any one
art in which they were excellent.

THOMAS LOVE PEACOCK (1785–1866), *Crotchet Castle*,
on the pretensions of Edinburgh as the 'Athens of the North'

It is said that a Scotchman returning home, after some years'
residence in England, being asked what he thought of the
English, answered: 'They hanna ower muckle sense, but they
are an unco braw people to live amang;' which would be a very
good story, if it were not rendered apocryphal, by the in-
credible circumstance of the Scotchman going back.

THOMAS LOVE PEACOCK (1785–1866), *Crotchet Castle*

Such Mediocrity was ne'er on view,
Bolster'd by tireless Scottish Ballyhoo –
Nay! In two qualities they stand supreme;
Their self-advertisement and their self-esteem.

ANTHONY POWELL (fl. C18th), 'Caledonia'

It requires a surgical operation to get a joke well into a Scotch understanding. Their only idea of wit, or rather that inferior variety of this electric talent which prevails occasionally in the north, and which, under the name of wut, is so infinitely distressing to people of good taste, is laughing immoderately at stated intervals.

SYDNEY SMITH (1771–1845), in Lady Holland,
Memorial of the Rev. Sydney Smith (1855)

God help England if she had no Scots to think for her.

GEORGE BERNARD SHAW (1856–1950)

There are some people who think they sufficiently acquit themselves, and entertain their company, with relating facts of no consequence, but at all out of the road of such common incidents as happen every day; and this I have observed more frequently among the Scots than any other nation.

JONATHAN SWIFT (1667–1745), *Hints Towards an Essay on Conversation*

Their beasts be generally small, women only excepted, of which sort there are none greater in the whole world . . . To be chained in marriage with one of them, were to be tied to a dead carcass, and cast into a stinking ditch; formosity and a dainty face are things they dream not of.

SIR ANTHONY WELDON,
A Perfect Description of the People and Country of Scotland (1617)

It is never difficult to distinguish between a Scotsman with a grievance and a ray of sunshine.

P.G. WODEHOUSE (1881–1975), in Richard Usborne,
Wodehouse at Work (1961)

Sports

Brissit brawnis and broken banis,
Stride, discord, and waistie wanis;
Crukit in eild, syne halt withal –
Thir are the bewties of the fute-ball.

Anonymous, 'The Bewties of the Fute-Ball'

Th'athletic fool to whom what Heav'n denied
Of soul is well compensated in limbs

JOHN ARMSTRONG (c. 1709–79), 'The Art of Preserving Health'

Tully produced a complimentary admission ticket from the waistband of his playing shorts during a game in which he was getting the better of his immediate opponent, the fearsome full-back Don Emery. He handed it to Emery, with the observation, 'Here, would you not be better watching from the stand?'

PETER BURNS and PAT WOODS, *Oh, Hampden in the Sun* (1997), on Charlie Tully, Celtic star of the late 1940s

In Glasgow, half the fans hate you and the other half think they own you.

TOMMY BURNS (1956–), quoted in Kenny MacDonald, *Scottish Football Quotations* (1994)

Ally MacLeod thinks that tactics are a new kind of mint.

> BILLY CONNOLLY (1942–), on the then Scotland
> soccer manager Ally MacLeod

Ally MacLeod

I support Partick Thistle. They'll be in Europe next year. If there's a war on.

> BILLY CONNOLLY (1942–), quoted in D. Campbell,
> *Billy Connolly: The Authorised Version* (1976)

My son was born to play for Scotland. He has all the qualities, a massive ego, a criminal record, an appalling drink problem. And he's not very good at football.

> 'MRS ALICE COSGROVE', quoted on the back cover
> of Stuart Cosgrove, *Hampden Babylon* (1991)

Because of televising around the world, Jim Watt fought for the world title at two in the morning. What they didn't know was that was to Jim's advantage. Everybody fights at two in the morning in Glasgow.

> TOMMY DOCHERTY (1928–)

Cricket is the only game where you can actually put on weight while playing.

TOMMY DOCHERTY (1928–)

He says, 'Who are you?' I says, 'Albion Rovers.' He says, 'Never heard of them.' I said, 'You ignorant bugger.' But it was a natural thing. I mean, it wisnae him alone – there were other people who'd never heard of Albion Rovers.

TOM FAGAN of Albion Rovers, in K. Macdonald,
Scottish Football Quotations (1994), on a 1985 FIFA meeting

They christened their game golf because they were Scottish and revelled in meaningless Celtic noises in the back of the throat.

STEPHEN FRY (1957–), *Paperweight*

Murray, a scowler of some distinction, often appears to have a chip the size of a girder on his shoulder. He swears at umpires, slags off the press, fumes on court, grimaces through TV interviews, appears to loathe his opponents, denigrates women's tennis and makes the sort of ill-advised comments guaranteed to alienate potential fans; in the run-up to the World Cup, he remarked that in the absence of Scotland he'd rather anyone except England won the tournament. Fair enough, I suppose, but not likely to win many friends from below the Border.

GQ magazine, November 2006,
on tennis player Andy Murray

. . . the Partick Thistle supporters' anthem goes like this:

> 'We hate Roman Catholics,
> We hate Protestants too,
> We hate Jews and Muslims:
> Partick Thistle we love you . . . '

ALASDAIR GRAY (1934–), 'The Trendelenburg Position',
in S. Maguire and D. Jackson Young, *Hoots* (1967)

There was a woman there with the blue eye-shadow and the red lipstick and I was walking off and she called me a big dirty Fenian bastard. I turned and said, 'Oh, come on,' and she said, 'Nothing personal, I know your Auntie Annie.'

TONY HIGGINS, striker for Hibernian FC,
in the BBC TV documentary *It's Only a Game* (1985)

Eck: . . . This is where I come to do what the Scots are best at.'
  Willie: Shinty?
  Eck: Moping.

JOHN MCKAY, *Dead Dad Dog* (1988)

Rabid and bigoted partisanship is an exceedingly mild term to apply to their ferocious ebulations. Were they of the working class there might be a little excuse for them, but the most of them at any rate are dressed like gentlemen. I am afraid the resemblance ends there. A worse exhibition than these gents favoured us with has not been given in Scotland. It was worthy of a band of drunken cannibals.

JOHN H. MACLAUCHLIN in the *Glasgow Examiner*,
1896, on Queen's Park supporters, the 'Hampdenites'

Slim Jim had everything required of a great Scottish footballer. Outrageously skilled, totally irresponsible, supremely arrogant and thick as mince.

> ALASTAIR MCSPORRAN in the fanzine *The Absolute Game* (1990), on the Rangers player Jim Baxter

Three things are thrown away on a bowling green, namely, time, money, and oaths.

> SIR WALTER SCOTT (1771–1832), *The Fortunes of Nigel*

He's got the heart of a caraway seed.

> BILL SHANKLY (1914–81), football manager, referring to a player he had just sold

After a lengthy goal famine had struck Scotland, it was rumoured that on one foreign trip, striker Gordon Durie couldn't find his way into the team hotel. Someone had painted goalposts over the door.

> TOM SHIELDS, *Tom Shields Too* (1993)

As a young Rangers player, Alex Ferguson . . . was unhappy at being left out of the first team. He stormed into the office of legendary manager Scott Symon. 'Why have I been in the second team for three weeks?' he asked. The magisterial Mr Symon replied, 'Because we don't have a third team.'

> TOM SHIELDS, *Tom Shields Too* (1993)

Shankly, who once played for a very minor Scottish team called Glenbuck Cherrypickers, is also alleged to have put his head round the door of the visitors' dressing room after a goalless game and announced, 'The better team drew.'

> BILL SHANKLY (1914–81), football manager,
> in W. Gordon Smith, *This Is My Country* (1976)

We do have the greatest fans in the world but I've never seen a fan score a goal.

> JOCK STEIN (1922–85), in A. Cran and J. Robertson,
> *A Dictionary of Scottish Quotations* (1996)

Reporter: So Gordon, any changes then?

Gordon Strachan: No, still Scottish, 5ft 6, ginger and a big nose!

> Attributed

Gary Lineker: So Gordon, if you were English, what formation would you play?

Gordon Strachan: If I was English I'd top myself!

> Attributed

Scott Harrison has pissed away a career then acted as if he is the victim. He doesn't have a chip on his shoulder, but a bag of King Edwards.

> FRANK WARREN, promoter, on the Scottish boxer after Harrison
> pulled out of his world title fight on 2 December 2006

People say that the Souness revolution was responsible for the rise in Rangers support but I think it's more to do with the Government Care in the Community policies, which threw these unfortunates onto the streets.

> IRVINE WELSH (1958–), interviewed on ErinWeb, 1997

Traditions and festivities

Hogmanay is about darkness. It is a ceremony based on the three 'Ds': the dark, the devil and the dram.

> Bruce Anderson, *The Sunday Telegraph*, 31 December, 2006

Edinburgh Festival audiences applaud everything with equal indiscrimination.

> Sir Thomas Beecham (1879–1961)

I deeply regret that we have not finished yet.

> Sir Thomas Beecham (1879–1961), to an Usher Hall audience that clapped prematurely (1956)

All that is desired is (1) to get some useful publicity; (2) make money; and (3) jack up a little the general illusion that the Scots are really a cultured people with an interest in the arts. In short, it is just another lousy racket.

> Hugh MacDiarmid (C.M. Grieve 1892–1978), *The Company I've Kept*, on the plan for the Edinburgh Festival

Dolly: That's whit ah like aboot this time o' the year, ye meet people ye've never met before.

Magrit: Aye . . . an usually ye hope ye'll never meet them again.

> Tony Roper, *The Steamie* (1987), on Hogmanay

Sin a' oor wit is in oor wame,
Wha'll flyte us for a lack o' lair;
Oor guts maun glorify your name
Sin a' oor wit is in oor wame.

WILLIAM SOUTAR (1898–1943),
'From Any Burns Club to Scotland',
on once-a-year Burnsians

People being sick on the pavement in Glasgow.

EVELYN WAUGH (1903–66),
Vile Bodies (1930), on Hogmanay

Travel and transport

I'm now arriv'd – thanks to the gods!
Thro' pathways rough and muddy:
A certain sign that makin' roads
Is no this people's study.
Altho' I'm not wi' Scripture cram'd,
I'm sure the Bible says
That heedless sinners shall be damn'd
Unless they mend their ways.

ROBERT BURNS (1759–96),
'Epigram on Rough Roads'

A worthy countryman who had come from the north-east side of the kingdom by train to Cowlairs, was told that the next stoppage would be Glasgow. He at once began to get all his little packages ready, and remarked to a fellow passenger, 'I'm sailin' for China this week, but I'm thinkin' I'm by the warst o' the journey noo.'

SIR ARCHIBALD GEIKIE (1835–1924),
Scottish Reminiscences

There was one the other day when the train was running along at its steady three miles an hour, and he tried to be funny. He said, 'I say, guard,' Fyffe enjoyed imitating the English and American accents – 'could I get out to pick a few flowers on the embankment while the train is in motion?' Oh, I was leerie for him. I said, 'If ye look oot, ye'll see there's nae flooers on this embankment.' 'Oh, that's all right,' said he, 'I've brought a packet of seeds.'

ALBERT D. MACKIE, *The Scottish Comedians* (1973),
on Will Fyffe's impersonation of a Highland Railway guard

The Day of Judgement is at hand when the MacBrayne steamer will be on time.

IAIN CRICHTON SMITH (1928–98), *Thoughts of Murdo*

Warfare

Ladies from Hell

> German description of kilted Scottish troops, World War I

Poison dwarfs

> German description of the Highland Light Infantry,
> during the post-World War II occupation of West Germany

> Ye hypocrites! are these your pranks?
> To murder men, and gie God thanks!
> For shame! Gie o'er – proceed no farther –
> God won't accept your thanks for murther.

ROBERT BURNS (1759–96), 'Verses Written on a Pane of Glass on the
Occasion of a National Thanksgiving for a Naval Victory'

They sent me word that I was like the first puff of a haggis,
hottest at the first.

SIR ROBERT CAREY, Warden of the March, of a message from the
Armstrongs in 1601, quoted in George MacDonald Fraser,
The Steel Bonnets (1971)

I have seen better-dressed and more capable dummies than
you outside cinemas.

Said to have been shouted on a megaphone by Captain Swanson
of the *St Ola* to the commander of Scrabster harbour in
World War II; recorded in Jo Grimond, *Memoirs* (1979)

There's some that we wan,
Some say that they wan,
Some say that nane wan at a', man;
But o' ae thing I'm sure,
That at Sherrifmuir,
A battle there was that I saw, man.
And we ran, and they ran,
And they ran, and we ran,
And they ran and we ran awa', man.

MURDOCH MACLENNAN (fl. early C18th), 'Sheriffmuir'

Hey! Johnnie Cope, are ye walkin' yet?
Or are your drums a-beating yet?
If ye were walking I wad wait
To gang to the coals in the morning!

ADAM SKIRVING (1719–1803), 'Johnnie Cope'

The captain's all right, really. A touch of the toasted teabreid.
You know the type.

W. GORDON SMITH, *Mr Jock* (1987)

Women

Women's patience – till you count three.

Gaelic proverb

They say in Fife
That next to nae wife,
The best thing is a gude wife.

Traditional

Though all the wood under heaven that grows
Were crafty pennis convenient for to write . . .
All the men were writtaris that ever took life
Could not write the false dissaitful despite
And wicketness contenit in a wife.

Anonymous, C16th

Here lyes a Maid not full sixteen,
Who was a servant to the Queen.
More men than years she had upon her,
But still she was a Maid of Honour.

Anonymous, C17th, 'On a Maid of Honour'

Here lyes enshrin'd in this foul lining
The mother of Jock and Willie Bining,
Who lived a miser, died ane witch,
And now to hell they hurl'd the bitch . . .
Her wynding sheet is ane old shirt,
Her funerall oyls are piss and dirt,
Her coffin is of ane old girnell,
Earth keeps the shell, the deil the kirnell.

Anonymous (C17th), in James Maidment's
Scottish Pasquils (1868), perhaps aimed at
William Binning, Provost of Edinburgh in 1676

 Why are the boys in blue so concerned about the women of the streets? I only ask because it seems Scotland's biggest force are patrolling the wrong beat – Whore Alley. Hookers are being molly-coddled by our police . . . Do tarts pay more council tax? Isn't protecting prostitutes a job for pimps? Are loose-living women, who choose to put themselves in harm's way, entitled to better protection than a decent wife . . .'

TOM BROWN, *Daily Record*, reported in
'Scottish Media Monitor', January 2001

She's fair and fause that causes my smart.

ROBERT BURNS (1759–96), 'She's Fair and Fause'

The Almighty made all things very good without doubt, but he left some mighty queer kinks in woman. But then the whole affair of her creation was an afterthought.

S.R. CROCKETT (1859–1914)

Until a woman is free to be as incompetent as the average male then she never will be completely equal.

ROSANNA CUNNINGHAM MP, in A. Cran and J. Robertson,
Dictionary of Scottish Quotations (1996)

She haunts the sculleries and parlours of Scotland's social history like an irreversible curse. She patrols our psyche like a bossy traffic warden . . . She is Black Agnes of the but-and-ben, scolding her men-folk, stiffening their backbone, sacrificing herself and her daughters on the altar of their incompetence.

JULIE DAVIDSON, *The Scotsman*, 19 February 1979,
on the Scottish mother-figure as personified by 'Ma Broon'

Today I pronunced a word that should never come out of a ladys lips it was I called John an Impudent Bitch.

MARJORY FLEMING (1803–11), *Journals*

Nature, I say, doth paynt them further to be weak, fraile, impacient, feble, and foolish; and experience hath declared them to be unconstant, variable, cruell, and lacking the spirit of counsel and regiment.

JOHN KNOX (c. 1505–72), *The First Blast of the Trumpet Against the
Monstrous Regiment of Women*

To promote a Woman to beare rule, superioritie, dominion or empire above any Realme, Nation or Citie, is repugnant to Nature; contumelie to God, a thing most contrary to his revealed will and approved ordinance, and finallie it is the subversion of good Order, of all equitie and justice.

JOHN KNOX (c. 1505–72), *The First Blast of the Trumpet Against the
Monstrous Regiment of Women*

Dear Douglas still maintains her Ground,
Empress of all the Bawds around;
(Where *Innocence* is often sold
For Hard Cash – for shining sordid Gold).
By Craft she draws the Money in,
And keeps a *Publick House* of Sin!

THOMAS LEGG (fl. C18th), *Covent Garden*,
on Jane 'Mother' Douglas, born Jane Marinet in Edinburgh

A Cattery of which the Principal Figure is a noted fat Covent Garden lady, Mother Douglas . . . a great flabby stinking, swearing hollowing ranting Billingsgate Bawd.

SIR CHARLES HANBURY-WILLIAM

The island women, on the whole, are plain; and many of them are exceedingly so. This applies to the young, as well as to the middle-aged and elderly.

ALASDAIR ALPIN MACGREGOR, *The Western Isles* (1949)

What is yon crew in the black ship, pulling her among the waves? A crew without fellowship, without sense, a disorderly minded band of women.

Let us leave on the stormy stream the the evil, leaky ship, and its load of noxious women, in the salt brine, without psalm or sea-creed.

THE McINTYRE BARD (C14th-15th), in W.J. Watson,
Scottish Verse from the Book of the Dean of Lismore (1937), from the Gaelic

She's a classy girl, though, at least all her tattoos are spelt right.

CHIC MURRAY (1919–85), *The Chic Murray Bumper Book*

. . . that mim-moothed snivellin' fule,
A fushionless woman.

DOROTHY MARGARET PAULIN (1904–), 'Said the Spaewife'

. . . the best opposite sex that men have got

JIMMY REID, *Glasgow Herald*, March 1981

They would have all men bound and thrall
To them, and they for to be free.

ALEXANDER SCOTT (c. 1520–c. 1590), 'Of Womankind'

Woman's faith and woman's trust:
Write the characters in dust.

SIR WALTER SCOTT (1771–1832), 'The Betrothed'

He worried about her, however, thinking that anyone who
would sleep with him would sleep with anybody.

IRVINE WELSH (1958–), *Trainspotting*

Index of insulters and insultees

(Note: authors of insults are in roman; subjects of insults are in *italic*. Scottish authors are indicated by an asterisk *)

BIRLINN LTD (incorporating John Donald and Polygon) is one of Scotland's leading publishers with over four hundred titles in print. Should you wish to be put on our catalogue mailing list **contact**:

Catalogue Request
Birlinn Ltd
West Newington House
10 Newington Road
Edinburgh EH9 1QS
Scotland, UK

Tel: + 44 (0) 131 668 4371
Fax: + 44 (0) 131 668 4466
e-mail: info@birlinn.co.uk

Postage and packing is free within the UK. For overseas orders, postage and packing (airmail) will be charged at 30% of the total order value.

For more information, or to order online, visit our website at **www.birlinn.co.uk**

Birlinn Limited
IMPRINTS: JOHN DONALD · POLYGON